May you be rich in LOVE & MONEY

Money
Is a Girl's
Best Friend

Money is a girl's best friend

How women can build up assets, trim debt and reap the rewards of being financially fit

Linda Leatherdale

turnerbooks.

TORONTO

Canadian Cataloguing in Publication Data

Leatherdale, Linda, 1953–
Money is a girl's best friend

ISBN 1-55228-014-4

1. Women—Finance, Personal. I. Title

HG179.L426 1998   332.024′042   C97-932802-0

We acknowledge the financial support of the Government of Canada through the Book Publishing Industry Development Program for our publishing activities.

turnerbooks.
1670 Bayview Avenue, Suite 310
Toronto, Ontario
M4G 3C2
(416) 489-2188

DESIGN: Pronk&Associates
COVER PHOTO: Silvia Pecota
AUTHOR'S MAKEUP AND HAIR: Gig
ILLUSTRATIONS: Tim Peckham
GRAPHICS: Harry Langford
PERSONAL FINANCE AND TAXATION FACTS VERIFIED BY:
Steve Ranot of Marmer Penner Inc.
INDEXING: Linda A. Fox

Printed and bound in Canada

98 99 00 01 6 5 4 3 2

Dedicated to my dear mother
Edith Ann Leatherdale,
from whom I learned love, compassion, and
respect for a buck.

Contents

FOREWORD
A Book For the Girls

Years ago, a somewhat chauvinistic suggestion was made about how women could net their riches. At the heart of it was a successful, well-to-do man— remember Hollywood starlet Marilyn Monroe and her haunting rendition of "Diamonds Are a Girl's Best Friend" in the movie *Gentlemen Prefer Blondes*?

Today, that myth is bunk, with many women climbing the corporate ladder and earning a key to the executive washroom as they share the career aspirations of their partners. Still, getting to the top is one tough feat, with boardrooms still dominated by males. And even when we do get there, chances are we're paid less.

When it comes to small businesses, statistics show women actually do a better job at operating a successful venture than their male counterparts. But again, the roadblocks are plentiful, an important one being securing start-up capital from the banks.

The sad reality is that even though many of us are getting business smarts and blossoming in our careers, when it comes to our financial affairs, some of us still aren't taking control. Part of the reason is that women tend to deal with money differently than men do. We're conservative and often feel uncomfortable with risk, while the guys like to be a little more daring. Some of us don't even get to handle the money, and when we suffer the blows of death or divorce, we feel totally helpless.

We have to face the facts: Up to 50% of marriages end in divorce, and as single mothers, our chances of living in poverty are even greater. Even if we don't divorce, it's likely we'll outlive our husbands. Facelifts or not, we're all getting older and we're all living longer. Witness Marie-Louise Meilleur, a Canadian who spent 117 years on this earth — and, who until she passed away on April 16, 1998, held the title as the world's oldest living woman. Then, there's a new World Health Organization study which predicts that by the year 2025, a child born in Canada will have a life expectancy of 81 years — the second longest of all nationalities on earth.

AGE NOW	LIKELIHOOD OF WOMEN LIVING BEYOND			
	80	85	90	95
65	69%	50%	29%	12%
70	74%	54%	31%	12%

Source: C.M. Oliver Financial Planning Corp.

Yet, while we're living longer, we're saving less, with Canada's personal savings rates at a record low. Making it tougher for the girls to save is the fact that we still earn only 71¢ for every dollar a male earns.

Meanwhile, total household debt in Canada, including credit cards, mortgages, personal loans, and auto debt, is now bigger than the federal government's net debt of $600 billion. That equates to more than 100% of real disposable income. No wonder personal bankruptcies remain at record levels, despite a recovering economy that continues to steam its way out of the Depression of the early 1990s.

When it comes to building that all-important nest egg, which will save us from living under the poverty line in our retirement years, some of us keep putting off getting started. Or, fearing the wild swings stock markets can suffer, we keep making silly investment mistakes, like keeping all our money in Canada Savings Bonds and Guaranteed Investment Certificates.

No one wants to live like a bag lady in their Golden Years. Yet, the reality is that 82% of retired women in Canada today need financial help from government, family, and friends just to get by. But unless we're prepared, there's a good chance we'll outlive our money and live in poverty after age 65.

That's why I wrote this book. It's for the girls, and it's aimed at showing that diamonds and rich men aren't necessarily the answer. We are. And we can be our own best friends when it comes to wealth creation.

This book is about how we can take charge. How to understand the good, the bad, and the ugly of credit. How to minimize risk while we seek out higher returns for our hard-earned savings. How to make our home an income stream. How to keep the taxman away. How to deal with financial implications of divorce. And how to keep our wealth, once we've created it.

There's no magic here, just good old common sense with the help of some well-thought-out financial planning.

The miracle is within you and your ability to chart a financial master plan and stick with it. So let's get started.

CHAPTER ONE

Taking Control

IT HAPPENED TO MOM, AND IT CAN HAPPEN TO YOU

Back in 1980, three weeks before my marriage, my father passed away from a massive heart attack. He was only 49. There were no warnings, no medical history of heart problems — just the aftershock that someone we loved so much, who had so much to live for could be taken away from us so early. Our family was devastated, not only emotionally, because he was such a strong leader in our lives, but we were also devastated financially, for we were forced to deal with things we never had to worry about before. While we scrambled to locate his last will, which we never found, his accounts were frozen, and I was left to pay for my own wedding.

But for my sweet, gentle mother, the shock was even harsher. For years, she had dedicated her life to raising her nine children and was an at-home mom, even though she had graduated from teachers' college with an honours degree and was a member of Toronto's Royal Conservatory of Music, where she gained the credentials to teach piano.

Never, never, had she been in control of the money. My father, who for years owned and operated a marina in the colourful Stephen Leacock's Mariposa town of Orillia in Ontario's cottage country, was the keeper of the funds. He simply gave her the money to buy the groceries and the clothes and to keep our household operating shipshape.

Now her whole world was about change.

In the end, good financial planning saved her. So did her piano and our mortgage-free home, which was originally built to house a tenant. The upstairs soon became an apartment, and it wasn't long before my mother became one of most popular, respected piano teachers in the land around Mariposa. We were, and still are, so proud of her.

Luckily, Mom had help from my brother-in-law, Ed, who works for an Orillia financial institution, and whose expertise was in investing. This being a family affair, his services were free. Believe me, we soon discovered that a good financial planner can make a lot of sense for many women.

As a child of the Great Depression, Mom had learned how to stretch a buck and needed no lessons about credit. She didn't believe in spending what you didn't have, and there was no massive debt she had to pay down. My father had re-invested his profits into his enterprise and, deservedly so, loved to enjoy the fruits of his labour, like owning an airplane. But it meant that Mom wasn't left with any huge pots of gold.

Back then, investing what she did inherit was a no-brainer. Interest rates were at record highs, with safe, interest-bearing vehicles like Canada Savings Bonds fetching an unbelievable 19%. The old magical formula of compound interest certainly worked, and Mom's conservative, no-risk nest egg started growing in leaps and bounds. Then she reaped the windfall of a sizeable inheritance from my grandfather, a pillar of the educational world, who had worked for years as an elementary school principal and who had helped to found Georgian College.

Now fast forward to the 1990s...and to one of the deepest economic contractions since the Great Depression. While economists were telling Mom low inflation and low interest rates would be good for her, the income stream from her nest egg was about to suffer one of its biggest blows as interest rates plunged to 30-year lows. While her bills, especially tax bills, continued to escalate, her income was cut in half. She also watched in horror as the value of her biggest asset, her home, suffered from deflation for the first time in post-war history. In other words, for the first time since the 1940s, the value of her home fell, instead of posting year-over-year gains.

On the phone to me, she would ask, "Linda, what should I do? The stock market scares me, but I can't live with these interest rates."

My mom was not alone in her anxiety. My mother-in-law, whose Presbyterian minister husband passed away from cancer seven years previously, faced the same dilemma. Being Depression babies who remembered stories of the Great Crash of 1929 when a stock market meltdown wiped out the life savings of many, they were scared. Certainly, sweet, conservative, religious women shouldn't be playing a crap shoot with the markets.

Or should they? Read on.

Mom really didn't start earning a penny on her own until Dad died. Sure, she ran the household budget—that is, she spent what money he gave her to buy food and clothing and to pay for the necessities, like trips to the dentist.

All of a sudden, not only was Mom in total control of the money, but she was also to become the key bread winner in her household. More and more women are facing this change in life, whether it's through death or divorce that we part from our spouses.

But even without death and divorce, our world has changed.

Remember the 1960s: We burnt our bras. We took the pill. We even, shock and horror, shacked up, instead of tying the knot. By the 1970s, we were exploding onto the job scene, seeking to make our own way in life, instead of spending our days cleaning the house, starching his shirts, changing diapers, and making his favourite meal at night in hope he'd share some of his exciting day with us during dinner conversation.

By the 1980s, fast food and TV dinners had overcome our dilemma of what to eat, and our dining conversation was about each other's day at work. But something else changed, too. More women were forced to go to work, thanks to inflationary spirals in home prices and taxation. Banks, all of a sudden, were lending money to buy homes based on two incomes, not one. Even though 48% of us working wives were now contributing 50% to the family's income, we were still being paid, on average, only 58% of what our male counterparts earned. And chances are, no matter how much money we brought in, we were still doing most, if not all, of the housework.

The 1990s, for many of us, proved to be brutal. Yes, we still faced the wage gap challenge, plus fights over who did the housework. But as re-engineering or corporate downsizing hit the landscape, our double-income families were going up in smoke. If we didn't lose a job, our husbands, live-ins, better halves, or whoever we share our lives with, did.

I know this well. On a cold, heartless, gray day in November 1996, the phone call came. I was in the shower, and even over the deafening sounds of streaming, steamy hot water, I could hear the shriek. "Linny, I'm on the list. I've lost my job," my husband stormed. I stood in shock as the hot water poured down on me, then I began to sob uncontrollably. I had never felt more lost, hurt, and humiliated.

We all knew bad news was coming at the *Toronto Sun*, where I work as Money Editor and my husband was employed as an assistant photo editor, and where management had warned us some serious cost cutting was needed to enhance the bottom line. More than 100 people met the same fate on that dark, dark day, and my heart goes out to them.

Losing a job, like losing a loved one, is a pain unbearable to endure, one that adds great stress to family life. In fact, according to the *Journal of Psychosomatic Research*, losing a job is one of the major stresses in life, next to death, divorce, or a major illness. But we cope. We become stronger. And we take control.

As my husband ventured into the world of self-employment, starting his own upscale woodworking company and never looking back, for me earning a good buck and securing my own future became more important than ever. So did money management. And so did retirement planning as my family lost one company pension while we stared bankrupt government pension plans in the face.

Many of us have experienced the same rude awakening. So now we're coming out of the closet even more. Our newest quest? Not only will we make money, but now we also want to make it grow, through our own wise investment strategies. Some of us even lust after millionaire status, just like the boys. Some of us have already made it. And in the new millennium, believe me, many more of us will.

ROLL OVER BEETHOVEN: IT'S TIME TO ROCK 'N' ROLL WITH THE GIRLS
One has only to look at some of the amazing returns being achieved by women's investment clubs to know females don't have to take a back seat to males when it comes to investing.

"Women can be very astute investors," comments Lorie Hamilton, director of personal trust services for Royal Trust, which conducted a study on investment trends of affluent women in Canada. "These women are not timid investors. They are confident investors who play an active role in managing household investments, and are not afraid to get the help they need in managing their finances."

Who are "they"? They are among Canada's top 10% households, with an annual income of $137,000. Their average age is 46, their household investment portfolio, excluding real estate, is $306,000, and their household net worth is $630,000. They have 1.3 children, and plan on retiring at age 58. Some 68% have estate plans, 73% plan to supplement Canada Pension Plan benefits, 67% have made plans to finance their children's education, 45% have separate investments outside an RRSP, and 86% say it makes no difference if their financial planner is male or female.

About one-third of these affluent women bring in at least half the household income and work more than 40 hours a week. One in five is a partner or an owner of a business. And before starting a business, 62% were employed by a corporation. These blue-chip women, though, do not necessarily feel warm and fuzzy about the blue-chip world. Lorie explains, "They believe corporations don't offer women the same opportunities for success as men." In other words, the old boys' network is alive and well. Meanwhile, new studies show the girls who made inroads in the 1980s into the corporate boardrooms of the nation have lost ground in the 1990s.

HIGH HEELS IN HIGH PLACES, BUT WHERE ARE
THE KEYS TO THE CORPORATE WASHROOM?

Even though, worldwide, more women hold managerial jobs than in the past, we still earn less than men and hold just 2% to 3% of the top jobs, reports a recent United Nations study. The report "Glass Ceiling" by the International Labor Organization shows women are prevented from getting to the top by an invisible male-dominated barrier (the old boys' network).

"Women today represent more than 40% of the global work force and have gradually moved up the hierarchical ladder of enterprises," the report says, "yet rarely does their share of management positions exceed 20%. The higher the position, the more glaring the gender gap."

In Canada, women make up 42% of the management spots, yet our management salaries for these positions are 68% of what our male counterparts earn.

Profile of the Executive Lady
- 30% are age 40 to 44; 22% are 35 to 39
- 6% are visible minorities
- 76% are married
- 65% have kids, 53% have kids under 18 at home
- 84% have partners employed full-time
- 54% earn $100,000 to $200,000 a year, 26% earn $200,000 to $400,000
- 87% provide at least half the family income.

Source: Closing the Gap Study

STILL GOT A LONG WAY TO GO, BABY

At the same time, statistics from Statistics Canada and the Canadian Women's Foundation underscored this: We've still got a long way to go, baby.

The good news, though, is the girls are finally closing the wage gap with the guys. In 1995, on average, we were earning 71¢ for every dollar a male earned. Back in 1990, we earned 67¢ on the dollar, and in 1980 it was 64¢. We also made strides in our purchasing power, with our average income increasing by 15% from 1980 to 1995, while the guys' average income fell 7.3%.

But the bad news is that the wage gap trend still exists in almost every category of Ottawa's latest census of incomes and earnings. And let's face it: Even though we've made some gains, our households were still shaken by an epidemic of falling incomes, not seen since the Great Depression. According to the census, some 21 million people in Canada had an average income of only $25,196, down 6% from 1990. That's less than the average income in 1980, meaning we're worse off now that we were 15 years ago, before our economy suffered the blows of corporate restructuring plus two recessions.

And, even with gains by the girls, men were still earning more in 1995, with an average of $31,117, compared to women at $19,208, even though more women were working and, by 1995, accounting for 49.7% of all people reporting income.

From judges, who on average are paid the most in Canada, to nannies, babysitters, and parents' helpers, who are the lowest paid, the wage gap trend was evident.

For example, the average income of a female judge was $117,707 in 1995, compared to a male judge, who earned $128,791. At the low end of the wage scale, a male nanny, parent helper, or babysitter averaged $15,106, while a female counterpart earned only $12,662.

Here are some more depressing statistics:

- Women's average annual pre-tax income in Canada in 1993 was $16,500, just 58% of men's average of $28,600.
- In 1993, 2.8 million women, or 20% of the total female population aged 15 and older, were living in low-income situations.
- Sixty percent of female lone parents in 1993 lived in low-income situations.
- Fifty-six percent of unattached senior women, aged 65 and older, have low incomes.

So what is a girl to do? Few of Canada's affluent women would ever suggest you go out and marry a rich man. Here's what the smart ones advise:

- **Get a good education.**
- **Start to save early.**
- **Get a good job and work hard.**
- **Be independent, manage your own money, and look after yourself.**
- **Set retirement goals.**

These are the million-dollar questions:

Even with less earning power and the possibilities of being a lone bread winner, can we avoid poverty when we retire? And can we become millionaires?

The answers: Yes, yes! Read on.

CHAPTER TWO

Wealth Strategies for the Girls

I NEED HOW MUCH TO RETIRE?

The numbers can leave any woman utterly speechless.

"I need how much to retire?" gasped my dear, sweet colleague, Linda Anne, a columnist at the *Toronto Sun* newspaper.

Linda Anne, who just turned 50, is a single working lady, who loves to spend her money on food and travel, and who easily admits her only real asset is her home, which is located in a desirable neighbourhood in Toronto.

When it comes to her former common-law partner, she spits nails. "To think I still owe him $30,000 for his investment in the house." The mortgage-free home—the biggest part of Linda Anne's nest egg—is worth about $220,000. But minus what she owes her ex, plus what she'll pay in real estate commission if she sells, the nest egg falls to $180,000.

This is scary stuff for Linda Anne when she keeps hearing that people in her income group will need a retirement nest egg of at least $1 million in order to live comfortably. "I didn't think it would happen to me," Linda Anne wrote in a recent column in the *Sun*, where she reported on a study by the Canadian Association of Retired Persons (CARP).

The study is called "The Black and Blue Book" and it quoted CARP president Lillian Morgenthau, who warned, "Canada may be one of the best places in the world to live, but it's fast becoming one of the worst places in the world for retirement." The book, written by Canada Pension Plan expert Walter Kelm, pointed out that over the years governments have clawed back Old Age Security benefits, changed tax exemptions that were formerly allowed based on age and retirement income, cut back the amount of RRSP contributions, and slashed health and social programs.

And let's not forget how Jean Chretien's Liberals were planning to hit us with a new Seniors' Benefit, which in year 2001 would combine the Old Age Security with the Guaranteed Income Supplement, to save government coffers $8.2 billion in pension money. This new benefit penalized the very Canadians who heeded Ottawa's advice and saved money for their own retirement.

For example, a couple who saved enough to enjoy an income of $78,000 a year would get zip in benefits, while facing an income tax rate of 45.8%; a couple with an income of $26,000 would see benefits clawed back by 20% and a 26% income tax hit.

"Here we had a government on one hand telling us to save for our own retirement," says Lillian, "then trying to penalize us for doing what they said."

CARP, and other groups like the Retirement Income Coalition, fought back, and the Liberals eventually backed off. But that doesn't mean the Seniors' Benefit may still not come back to haunt us.

Meanwhile, the three traditional pillars of Canada's retirement system still stand:

- Old Age Security/Guaranteed Income Supplement, automatically paid at age 65.
- Canada Pension Plan (CPP), also paid at age 65, although scaled-back early CPP benefits can be set up at age 60.
- RRSPs.

But even with these pillars, 30% of Canadians who retired in 1996 were living below the poverty line. And even though seniors are getting $6 in benefits for every $1 they put in, it's only going to get worse from here. Baby boomers will be lucky to get a dollar for every dollar they put in, while Generation Xers could be the big losers.

The bottom line remains: For most of us, the only thing that will keep us from poverty in old age will be the amount of money we socked away during our working years. Yet most recent studies show that although about 57% of us plan on living off our RRSPs, only about 22% of us are contributing annually. And worse, the average yearly contribution is a mere $4,000.

Also, 63% of Canadians do not have the luxury of company pension plans, which are going the way of the dinosaur. A survey by the Canadian Imperial Bank of Commerce shows the sources of income that Canadians expect to retire on:

Sources of Retirement Income Canadians are Counting On
- 57% — RRSPs
- 33% — Company pension plans
- 32% — Canada Pension Plan
- 13% — Other non-RRSP money
- 9% — Employment or other income
- 8% — Non-financial assets
- 5% — Inheritances

Warnings from CARP president Lillian Morgenthau sent chills down Linda Anne's spine: "We're seeing a steady increase in the number of retirees who are having trouble managing," she said. "People are living longer and spending many more years in retirement than ever before, so they must plan very carefully."

The blood drained from Linda Anne's face. "I only began investing in RRSPs five years ago."

So can Linda Anne catch up?

"It's never too late to get aggressive," claims financial planner Steven Pearl of C.M. Oliver Financial Planning Corp. Steven took a closer look at Linda's financial picture, and the good news is Linda Anne is better off than she thought. Linda Anne's big advantage is that she's one of the few working women to enjoy a company pension plan. In fact, while women make up almost 45% of Canada's paid labour force, 61% work in jobs that don't provide pensions. Linda Anne is lucky. If she remains a loyal employee until age 65, her annual company pension will be $21,600.

She'd also forgotten about some assets she'd accumulated over the years. Her collectibles, including art, are valued at about $10,000.

Then there are the RRSPs she began contributing to five years ago. At $5,000 a year, this nest egg had grown to $34,000. Linda Anne, normally a very conservative investor, had expanded her portfolio into mutual funds, some of them equity-based. The returns from a record high stock market were very impressive.

If the cash-strapped Canada Pension Plan is still around by the time Linda Anne retires, she will receive $8,725 a year. She'll also get another $4,728 through Old Age Security.

When Steven finally crunched all the numbers, based on an income tax rate of 33.3%, an inflation rate of 3.2%, and a return on investments of 9%, Linda Anne was in for a pleasant surprise.

All she'd need to sock away from age 50 to 65 was $3,005 a year, or $250 a month in order to accumulate a big enough nest egg to give her 70% of her earned income.

The picture was even better if she continued with her $5,000-a-year RRSP contribution. Then she'd net a surplus of $73,068 for incidentals, like a new car, vacations, etc.

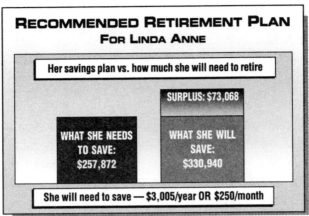

RECOMMENDED RETIREMENT PLAN
FOR LINDA ANNE

Her savings plan vs. how much she will need to retire

SURPLUS: $73,068

WHAT SHE NEEDS TO SAVE: $257,872

WHAT SHE WILL SAVE: $330,940

She will need to save — $3,005/year OR $250/month

"I'm so relieved," she sighed, as the fear of living below the poverty line vanished. But Linda Anne confessed she may not want to work until age 65. Even if she was to retire at age 60, she could still manage it, says Steven, but it would be tougher. "What she is doing is shortening the period of compound interest," he explains.

If Linda Anne wants to stop working in 10 years, she'd need to put away $14,105 a year, or $1,175 a month. That would give her a nest egg of $351,237, which would return anywhere from 63% to 70% of the paycheque she enjoys today. If she was to invest only $5,000 a year, and she decided to give up work at age 60, she'd be living off a nest egg that would give her only 45% of today's paycheque since the company pension payments are reduced when you take early retirement. "Linda Anne would be changing her lifestyle, for sure," quips Steven.

But what about Freedom 55, and that dream to tell the boss to stuff it 10 years before the traditional retirement age of 65? Steven explained to Linda Anne that the only hope of Freedom 55 is to win the lottery.

Linda Anne is lucky enough to have a company pension plan. But what about those who don't? Let's say you've been earning an income of $38,000 a year. Most experts will agree you'd need a nest egg of some $750,000 in order to enjoy the life you've become accustomed to.

The following charts offer more estimates:

How Much Will You Need When You Retire?[*]

To Produce an annual income of:	For a life expectancy beyond age 65 of:		
	10 years	20 years	30 years
	You Need to Save		
$30,000	$519,030	$768,291	$1,137,258
$40,000	$692,040	$1,024,338	$1,516,344
$50,000	$865,049	$1,280,484	$1,895,430

[*] Based on a 4% inflation rate

As to how Linda Anne should shape her portfolio, Steven suggests that, given her age and the kind of returns she needs, it should be balanced. "I'd put about 60% in equities (shares or stocks), 40% in fixed income, like government bonds, T-bills, stripped bonds, or even GICs," he said. But would Steven still advise so much money in equities if there was a stock market meltdown?

He says yes. Read on.

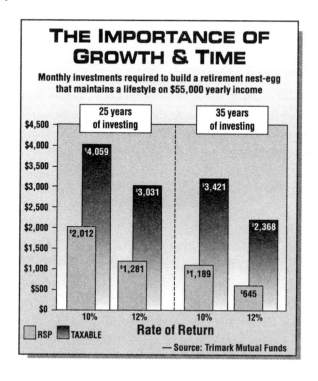

THE IMPORTANCE OF GROWTH & TIME

Monthly investments required to build a retirement nest-egg that maintains a lifestyle on $55,000 yearly income

— Source: Trimark Mutual Funds

SNOOZE, YOU LOSE

Why is it that some girls think of wealth as a dirty word?

"What's the point of saving any money? I'm going to have to work my whole life anyway," sighed Erica, the daughter of a friend, voicing the frustrations of many in what's dubbed the Echo Generation. "You guys (she means aging baby boomers) have had it all your way, and now we'll be made to pay."

Erica's sentiment reflects what many young people feel—that they'll be left with no future, no chance to build up wealth as they face the huge tax and debt consequences left behind by a generation that lived the great life. Besides, to this 20-year-old, a financial plan is the last thing she wants to think about. An outing to the mall is far more exciting. Erica is about to make a fatal mistake.

Canadians' attitude towards wealth creation can easily be summed up with these statistics:

Let's say 100 women who began to work at age 25 retired at age 65. Here's where they'd be:

- **Eighty-two women would need financial help from government, family, and friends.**
- **Eleven women would be working whether they want to or not.**
- **Four women would be dead.**
- **Two women would be enjoying a lifestyle close to what they had when they worked.**
- **One woman would be wealthy.**

The key to wealth creation is our attitude and our drive to make dreams come true. If Erica sees herself in diamonds, retired on a yacht in the Riviera, or sitting behind an oak desk making million-dollar decisions and helping to make people's lives better by offering them gainful employment, it will happen.

But without that drive and dream, and the ability to see ourselves there, forget it. We'll just ride the tide with the rest of the hangers-on.

MILLIONAIRE'S ROAD MAP

Most goals in life are achieved through a master plan, so if you desire the good life, then set out to make that dream come true.

Erica is young. Her golden opportunity lies at her feet. For example, at 20, if she began to put just $1 a day or $365 a year into a Registered Retirement Savings Plan (see Chapter 3) that earned on average 15% annually, she'd have almost $2 million when she retired at age 65. And that's without a rich man.

Now let's say she was to invest $1,000 a year and, playing the riskier investments, she was able to net an average annual return of 20%. By age 65, she'd have almost $5 million.

This is powerful stuff. This is the kind of stuff that makes millionaires. And it can happen, when we start young enough, stick to our plan, and learn how to pay ourselves first. Even if we start investing when we're young, then stop, maybe due to financial reasons, we're still further ahead than we would be if we'd started later in life.

Let's see what can happen if Erica begins to invest $2,000 a year at age 19 and does so every year until age 26, then never contributes again. Guess what? With an average growth rate of 10% annually, she'd end up with $1,035,160 by age 65.

But let's say she waited until age 27 to start investing $2,000 a year at 10%, and she did so faithfully until age 65. By the time she retired, she'd have only $883,185.

The Importance of Compounding & Time

Based on 10% growth rate

Age	INVESTOR A Annual Investment	Year-End Value	INVESTOR B Annual Investment	Year-End Value
19	2,000	2,200		0
20	2,000	4,620		0
21	2,000	7,282		0
22	2,000	10,210		0
23	2,000	13,431		0
24	2,000	16,974		0
25	2,000	20,872		0
26	2,000	25,159		0
27		27,675	2,000	2,200
28		30,442	2,000	4,620
29		33,487	2,000	7,282
30		36.835	2,000	10,210
31		40,519	2,000	13,431
32		44,571	2,000	16,974
33		49,028	2,000	20,872
34		53,930	2,000	25,159
35		59,323	2,000	29,875
36		65,256	2,000	35,062
37		71,781	2,000	40,769
38		78,960	2,000	47,045
39		86,856	2,000	53,950
40		95,541	2,000	61,545
↓		↓	↓	↓
60		642,753	2,000	540,049
61		707,028	2,000	596,254
62		777,731	2,000	658,079
63		855,504	2,000	726,087
64		941,054	2,000	800,896
65		1,035,160	2,000	883,185
Total Invested		**$16,000**		**$78,000**
Value of Investment		**$1,035,160**		**$883,185**
Money Grew		**64 fold**		**10 fold**

Source: Trimark Mutual Funds

But even if we're not as young as Erica and we're age 50, like my columnist friend Linda Anne, we can still do it. The trick is to sit down and map out where we are, where we want to be, and how we can get there. And that, as any financial planner worth his or her salt will tell you, starts with a chart of your net worth, or a look at where you are now.

How Much Are You Worth?

Calculating your net worth is simple. First you must list what you own: For example, what's in your chequing or savings accounts? What real estate, mutual funds, bonds, stocks, etc., do you own? Do you have a pension plan? Then list your personal possessions. What property or furniture do you own? How about jewellery, art, or collectibles? Any other assets? (No, you can't list your adorable boyfriend.) Now tally up the total value of your assets. That's one side of the score sheet.

On the other side of the score sheet will be what you owe, and I bet—like a good workout—this will make you sweat. Here you list those bad things, called credit cards, and unpaid bills, investment loans, and mortgages. Now tally up your total debt. Your net worth, plus or minus, will be the difference between what you own or have in investments and what you owe.

The following Net Worth chart will help you work it out.

How To Calculate Your Net Worth

Assets
What You Own:
A. Savings and investments

Chequing Accounts	_____
Savings Accounts	_____
GICs	_____
Mutual Funds	_____
Stocks	_____
Bonds	_____
Real Estate	_____
RRSPs/Pension Plan	_____
Cash Surrender Value of Life Insurance	_____
Mortgages At Principle Value	_____

Total Investment Assets $_____

B. Personal Possessions:

Property/Furniture	_____
Jewellery/Art/Collectibles	_____
Other Personal Assets	_____

Total Personal Assets $_____

Total Assets $_____

What You Owe:

Credit Cards	_____
Unpaid Bills	_____
Car Loans	_____
Other Loans	_____
Investment Loans	_____
Business Loans	_____
Other Debts	_____
Mortgages	_____

Total Liabilities $_____

Total Assets Minus Total Liabilities = Your Net Worth $_____

Now that you've found out where you are, the next question you must ask yourself is where you want to be. If you have a target of, let's say, $1 million by age 65, then you have to decide how to get there. For most of us, that means investing our money. And that, in turn, means finding out about the stock market, mutual funds, bonds, and other investment products, as well as how to diversify portfolios and enjoy the rewards of compounding growth.

It also means learning this wise investment rule: Learn how to pay yourself first. This is very simple, just like paying a monthly debt (car payments, personal loan, or a mortgage). But instead of paying a creditor, like the bank, you pay yourself by saving whatever you can afford from each paycheque and investing the money.

Sometimes employers will offer automatic payroll deduction plans, in which a designated amount of money is taken from each paycheque and invested in a group RRSP. Or you can arrange to have the bank shave off a certain amount from each paycheque and apply the money to the investment of your choice. You can also arrange for a financial planner or broker to do the same.

THE WEALTH CHART: "I'LL TAKE YOU THERE."

Time and time again, I remind investors that the economy swings in cycles, and patterns repeat themselves. What's interesting is how, through stock market highs and crashes, equities or shares will outperform all other investments. If you want to become wealthy, shares in the long term can get you there.

My husband's aunt, a kind, lovable 82-year-old retired schoolteacher, knows this well. Aunt Mae, who never married and still resides in the family home on a pleasant, quiet, tree-lined street in New Glasgow, Nova Scotia, started investing in the stock market after she landed her first teaching job in the 1940s. Back then, she earned a mere $600 a year, but understood that if she paid herself first, she'd never have to worry in her retirement years.

With each paycheque, she bought a stock. And being conservative, as most women are when it comes to investing, she stuck to blue-chip shares, mainly utilities like phone companies. First, it was Maritime Tel & Tel, then Bell Canada, then some bank stocks, whose values almost double every seven years and offer handsome regular dividend cheques. She even bought war-time savings bonds.

Aunt Mae believed in diversification and balance. She wasn't afraid to seek help from a financial planner. And she knew, in the long term, good-performing shares would strengthen her portfolio, which for her over the years included safe, boring Guaranteed Investment Certificates (GICs), when interest rates were good.

Women shouldn't be afraid of equities or stocks, even through the peaks and valleys of bull and bear markets. (A bull market, by the way, is one where share values keep heading higher. A bear is the opposite.) And here's why.

Let's say Aunt Mae had $10,000 in 1950, and she invested it in the stock market. By 1993, with an average annual return of 11.3%, her $10,000 would grow to $739,408. And that included the Great Stock Market Crash of October 19, 1987.

Now let's say Aunt Mae took another $10,000 and invested it in long-term bonds, which offer growth but not the same degree of risk. Her $10,000 by 1993 would grow to $154,500, a 6.8% return.

Then, Aunt Mae took another $10,000 in 1950 and socked it into safe Treasury bills. After 33 years, it would have grown only to $137,400, a 6.6% return.

The Wealth Chart

Here's how $1 grew, when invested in 1950 over a 40-year period:
- Common stocks (based on the TSE index) $71.68
- Treasury Bills $13.45
- Government Bonds $11.49

A further breakdown shows that over a 40-year history of the Toronto Stock Exchange, the average return for a one-year investment was 11.5%. If the money was left in for five years, the return was 10.2%, and over ten years, it averaged 10.17%. Still, stocks can still send shivers down the spines of even the most daring women. Here's why.

THE GREAT STOCK MARKET MELTDOWN: BLACK MONDAY, OCTOBER 27, 1997
What Mom, my friend Linda, and other conservative, nervous investors feared in the darkest corners of their minds finally happened in the fall of 1997. After more than two years of hearing doomsayers warn investors the sky was falling, the Great Stock Market Meltdown hit.

The day was Black Monday, October 27, 1997. I was on the set of CITY TV's "Before Breakfast Television" at 6:30 a.m., with handsome news anchor Kevin Frankish, when it hit home that, finally, this could be the real thing. Halfway around the world, in Hong Kong, the all-important Hang Seng index had plummeted by another 5.8%, after shedding 10% of its value a week earlier and sending shock waves around the world. In Asia, where a banking crisis loomed, the market bloodbath was brutal, as the fear of higher interest rates threatened corporate profits. But, so far, the record-high North American markets had held up.

Not this Monday.

By the time lunch rolled around, brokers were phoning their creditors and handing over the keys for their leased Jags and Mercedeses. The day of reckoning on Bay Street and Wall Street had arrived. By 3:30 p.m., after both the Toronto and New York stock exchanges suffered their worst one-day plunge in history, the circuit breakers were triggered and trading was halted. The TSE's all-important 300 composite index had crashed by 434.4 points, the Dow Jones industrial average, by 554.26. Political leaders and financial gurus on both sides of the border were busy calming the frayed nerves of anxious investors everywhere, who had socked billions of dollars into the high-flying stock markets.

But the difference between this meltdown and the Great Market Crash of October 19, 1987, was that this time the loss in paper value wasn't as painful.

This time, the Dow lost only 7.2% of its worth, and the TSE, 6.1%—which seemed insignificant when stacked against the record gains these exchanges had enjoyed during the longest-running bull market in our history.

Still, these haunting questions remained. Would markets now be on a road to further crashes? And could some doomsayers, warning of a meltdown of values of up to 80%, be right?

My phone lines at the *Sun* and on my "Moneyline" TV show were burning up.

"Linda, I listened to the advice of your experts last year and I cashed out my best performing stocks. I've been sitting liquid and waiting for this to happen," remarked a faithful viewer of my show. She couldn't wait for the markets to re-open so she could buy back some solid, blue-chip stocks at bargain-basement prices.

Another caller quipped she wasn't fazed by the crash. "My adviser tells me not to panic, so I'm not," she stated confidently, adding her financial plan was for long-term investing, and she wasn't going to get caught up in market swings and hype.

Good for her.

Back at the *Sun*, a pleasant voice mail was waiting. It was from John Kurgan, a futures expert who'd been a guest on my show a year earlier, and who, with his youthful, charming appearance, looked more like a Sunshine Boy than a stiff, buttoned-down Bay Street type.

"Look up your column of May 1," his voice mail urged. I did and I chuckled.

Here was a guy who, like economist Jeff Rubin of Wood Gundy, had the guts to call a market swing, despite the ridicule he would suffer from colleagues, bosses, and the public at large. Rubin's claim to fame was the accuracy with which he predicted the Great Real Estate Crash of 1989, when nobody wanted to see it coming.

Kurgan, armed with sophisticated research of trading patterns, wasn't afraid to speak out on a stock market meltdown.

But unlike others, who in slick newsletters were urging clients to sell, sell, sell and who were possibly looking to line their own pockets, this guy wasn't after money. Nor was he after media hype, and the fame it could bring. He simply believed that what runs too hot will sooner or later turn cold. And he wanted to warn investors if they followed the herd, if they bought at the top, then panicked and sold at the bottom, they'd end up a lamb chop.

Several columns that I wrote proved Kurgan was right. One showed an interesting pattern tied to U.S. presidential elections and how unlucky the number seven can really be.

Kurgan's data, which tracks the performance of the New York Stock Exchange's key indices, dates back to 1890. From 1890 to 1899, he tracked the Dow Rails, one of these key indices. From 1900, he tracked the Dow Jones industrial average. His data clearly revealed a pattern in which the seventh year of every decade spooked stock markets. He warned 1997 would be no different.

In fact, Kurgan's research showed the seventh year following a U.S. presidential election was even worse. This meant a double whammy in 1997, one year after Bill Clinton again won the hearts of Americans and was returned to the White House.

History speaks for itself. In 1917, the Dow lost 22% of its value after the 1916 election of President Woodrow Wilson. In 1937, one year after President Franklin Roosevelt was elected, it dropped 33%. In 1957, the loss was 13%, a year after the election of President Dwight Eisenhower. And in 1977, one year after voters put President Jimmy Carter in the White House, the Dow lost 17% of its value.

Kurgan stood behind his research and gut feeling. He was one day off calling the markets' record high in 1997, and he was right on calling for a 10% correction in the spring of 1997. He also warned that after the spring correction, many investors would be lulled into the false sense that the worst was over and they could get caught up in greed as markets hit new record highs over summer. Again, he was right. Most of us kept socking money in at record highs, while Kurgan was warning the real thing (a meltdown) would likely hit in late October or the first of November. And it did.

So, are the markets really for everyone, including Linda, Erica, Aunt Mae, and my own sweet, conservative mom, whose every cent counts?

Keep reading.

WHAT A DIFFERENCE A DAY MAKES

The day following Black Monday, October 27, 1997, I was with TV anchor Kevin Frankish again. This time, as he interviewed me, I sat on the edge of a desk and with hands clasped and eyes closed, I said a little prayer for our stock markets. My deepest fear was the bloodbath would continue when North American markets re-opened for trading, and that the little investor would be hurt.

But John Kurgan was right again. When I finished my TV stint by 7 a.m., and was back in my office at the *Sun*, the telephone rang.

"I think the markets are going to bounce back, but I'll call you back," said Kurgan, who obviously worked the same ungodly hours I did. By noon, Kurgan was on the line again. "It's happening," he gushed, "the markets are coming back." By the end of the day, the TSE had recovered an amazing 137 points to close at 6736. And on Wall Street, the Dow Jones was up 328 points to close at 7489.

With a big sigh of relief, brokers were asking for a return of the keys to their luxury cars.

What's the lesson here?

SHORT-TERM PAIN, LONG-TERM GAIN?

After many years of investing in stocks, Aunt Mae already knows this: Stocks can suffer short-term pain, but in the end they offer long-term gain.

Let's take a closer look. Let's say Mom put $10,000 into the Toronto Stock Exchange back in September 1982 and held on until September 1997, ignoring the Great Stock Market Meltdown of October 19, 1987. Guess what? Her return on her money would be an impressive 13.88%, with her $10,000 growing to $70,059.

The Magic of Markets

(Based on an initial $10,000 investment and factoring in the effect of compounding)

TSE 300

Month End	Market Value	% Change
09/82	$10,000	0.00
12/82	$12,371	23.71
12/83	$16,761	35.49
12/84	$16,360	-2.39
12/85	$20,461	25.07
12/86	$22,293	8.95
12/87	$23,604	5.88
12/88	$26,219	11.08
12/89	$31,823	21.37
12/90	$27,114	-14.80
12/91	$30,372	12.02
12/92	$29,936	-1.43
12/93	$39,680	32.55
12/94	$39,610	-0.18
12/95	$45,365	14.53
12/96	$58,224	28.35
12/97	$70,059	20.33

Average annual return: 13.8

Now, if Mom had headed to New York City and put her money into the Dow Jones industrial average, during the same 15-year period, she would have enjoyed a 20.84% return. And that means the same $10,000 would have grown to $164,847.

The Magic of Markets
(Based on an initial $10,000 investment and factoring in the effect of compounding)

Dow Jones

Month End	Market Value	% Change
09/82	$10,000	0.00
12/82	$11,755	17.55
12/83	$14,986	27.48
12/84	$16,154	7.79
12/85	$22,726	40.69
12/86	$28,530	25.54
12/87	$28,308	-0.78
12/88	$30,116	6.38
12/89	$38,498	27.83
12/90	$38,382	-.30
12/91	$47,507	23.77
12/92	$56,092	18.07
12/93	$68,278	21.73
12/94	$75,999	11.31
12/95	$101,135	33.07
12/96	$130,812	29.34
12/97	$164,847	26.02

Average annual return: 20.54

But Mom, like so many women, preferred the safety of GICs. So instead her $10,000 grew to $38,412, giving her an average return of 9.39%.

How GICs Fared
(Based on an initial $10,000 investment and factoring in the effect of compounding)

Month End	Market Value	% Change
09/82	$10,000	0.00
12/82	$10,297	2.97
12/83	$11,541	12.08
12/84	$12,998	12.63
12/85	$14,468	11.31
12/86	$15,937	10.15
12/87	$17,534	10.03
12/88	$19,387	10.57
12/89	$21,484	10.82
12/90	$24,008	11.74
12/91	$26,326	9.66
12/92	$28,426	7.98
12/93	$30,305	6.61
12/94	$32,627	7.66
12/95	$35,009	7.30
12/96	$37,057	5.85
12/97	$38,412	3.66

Average annual return: 9.39

This is interesting: What if Mom had got real aggressive with her money, and sent it halfway around the world to invest in the stock market in Hong Kong? Ready for this? Her $10,000 would be worth $270,253, for a return of 24.58%.

The irony here is that it was Hong Kong's Hang Seng index that sent our record-high stock markets in North America tailspinning into their biggest point crash since 1929. And even more ironic? After leading the bloodbath, which scared the life out of many hard-working people who simply want to build up a retirement nest egg so they can live their final years in peace, the Hang Seng was back on a roll again.

In the few days following the Great Crash of October 1997, the Hang Seng skyrocketed, giving investors another 18.5% return. For those with the stomach for playing market swings, that's easy money.

But it's tough stuff, believe me. Because since then, we've been living in the horror of an Asian flu and financial crisis that's wiped out banks and brokerage houses, sending world stock markets and currencies on a roller coaster ride.

One doomsayer who really suffered a lot of ridicule for his great crash rants, Bay Streeter Mark Borkowski, still believes more fallout is on the way. He was right.

Mark, president of Mercantile Mergers & Acquisitions, was scorned and laughed at when, in late 1996, he predicted a mammoth meltdown, triggered by the collapse of some Japanese financial powerhouses, which would spark a crisis here on North American soil. As a guest on my "Moneyline" show, Borkowski was mocked so badly that one viewer called in and quipped, "Bre-X should be drilling holes in your head." On my final show before we broke for summer 1997, Borkowski was made to eat crow (okay, it was a barbecued chicken). The majority of callers gonged him, because they didn't want to believe a crash was coming.

In the end, we were the ones eating crow as we watched our dollar plunge to new record lows and saw the International Monetary Fund bail out some Asian countries. Borkowski's predictions were off by more than a year. But the crash happened, ending the longest-running bull market in history.

Three weeks after the Stock Market Meltdown, Japan's largest brokerage house—Yamaichi Securities—failed, leaving behind some $24 billion in liabilities. At the Tokyo Stock Exchange, Yamaichi president Shohei Nozawa choked back tears as he apologized to investors, "It breaks my heart that the situation has turned out like this." It was the biggest business failure in Japan since the Second World War. Yamaichi was also the third Japanese financial company to fail in less than a month. Sanyo Securities, a medium-sized brokerage, went bankrupt on November 3. Then a week later, Japan's eleventh-largest commercial bank, Hokkaido Takushoku, collapsed. And the fallout continued.

Market analyst Ross Healy, president of Strategic Analysis Corp., believes the bears have finally taken over North America's record bull markets, and that the bears will reign for at least a year as over-valued stocks give themselves a reality check. Making it even more confusing is the fact that as we continued to suffer a series of mini corrections in spring 1998, our markets continued to rock 'n' roll to new record highs. Who ever thought we'd have a record 9000 Dow Jones one day, then a plunge of 150 points the next, and then a new record high? It's like taking a thrilling bungee jump.

How long will the Asia flu last? As this book goes to press, more mayhem is hitting. The TSE, after hitting new record highs in April 1998, is suffering a bigger correction than October 1997. The Canadian dollar has hit new record lows, falling into US64¢ territory, and the Bank of Canada finally raised interest rates, as the economy appears to be faltering. These are troubled times.

For the smart woman who dares to try to time the market, this could present some decent buying opportunities. But for most of us, who don't have the stomach or are close to retirement, it may mean battening down the hatches or switching some investments to safe liquid assets. The guide should be your risk tolerance, your age, and identifying and using a strategy that works for you. But remember: Nobody became a millionaire without a little risk.

FEAR AND GREED: THE EVIL TWINS

I like to think of Toronto lawyer Glorianne Stromberg as the wise grandmother of the securities industry, who in a gentle but firm manner knows how to share her wisdom and watch over her children so that all is right in their world.

I mean that Stromberg, a sweet, brilliant lady who sat as an Ontario Securities commissioner for 15 years, was determined that nobody would lead us astray when it came to this new explosive industry called financial services. Her enemies? Anyone who evoked the emotions of fear and greed to drive the naive or the novice into making wrong investment decisions.

"The best tool for anyone making investment decisions is knowledge," says Glorianne, who in her famed Stromberg Report urged better disclosure from mutual fund companies on information such as fees, commissions, and rates of returns.

As an OSC commissioner, Glorianne also sought tighter controls for financial planners, who in most provinces work with few or no regulations in place. She recites over and over the Golden Rule that governs anyone selling an investment product. That rule is "Know your client."

In other words, we all have a right to be fully informed about the product we're buying and the right not to be exposed to a sales tactic encouraging us to buy something that we'd stay up all night and worry about. Thanks, Glorianne, for your guiding light, and dedicated work that's led to a new code of ethics for mutual funds salespeople in Ontario.

One of the best examples of how fear and greed can take over is Bre-X, that bankrupt Canadian junior gold mining stock that stole the life savings of many a folk.

While the best-selling, soap-opera saga of Calgary-based Bre-X made some astute book authors some money and lined the pockets of those who know how to play the game, it unfortunately lost millions for innocent investors who got caught up in the hype. Even the media, blinded by the glitter of fool's gold, bought this sucker hook, line, and sinker.

Bre-X, with its misleading propaganda of the world's largest gold find in Indonesia and soap-opera story line that included rumours of murder, made Canada look silly on the international stage and brought home an urgent message that our limp-wristed securities rules need to be tightened up. There was no gold, just a scheme, or should I say scam, to make some people rich.

The industry calls this "pump and dump" and here's how it works. Promoters "pump" or promote the stock as a real winner, sending values up and up. Then, when the value hits a high, they "dump" or sell the stock and take their profits, before the unsuspecting public learns it was a dud and loses money.

Believe me, for those who pump, the promoters and insiders, the rewards can be awesome. The rewards can also be awesome for the smart player who bought the hype, got in at the bottom, and knew to sell before the hype blew up into little pieces of worthless paper.

But sadly, hype works when fear and greed take over. The fear is if they sell, they'll lose out on new highs. And the greed is "I want more, more, more."

"I've lost most of my savings," cried an elderly lady who phoned into my "Moneyline" show. "How can this happen to me?" Many others want an answer to the question, too.

The bottom line is yes, junior capital stocks—sometimes known as penny stocks, nickel deals, blind pools—can play an important role in raising precious capital for fledgling firms. And the rules cannot be too strict to deter that. But the reality is that too many pumpers are out there for the sole purpose of taking advantage.

It's no wonder my sweet mother, like so many others, cast a wary eye at high-flying stocks and the greed they can evoke.

Today, not only are we dealing with Bre-X fallout, and an Asian banking crisis, but now we also hear the FBI has made arrests over stock price manipulation that involved the Mafia, not only in the United States, but in Japan, too.

We've also watched as an over-zealous London, Ontario, financial advisor was stripped of his licence to sell financial instruments by the Ontario Securities Commission, after he bilked investors for $2.8 million by flogging bogus limited partnerships that invested in Italian cow embryos.

Live by this rule, and you won't get burned: "If it's too good to be true, it's not true." Just like men who say, "Trust me."

MUTUAL FUNDS: A MUTUALLY SATISFYING AFFAIR

The mutual fund craze took Canada by storm. "Give me some of those investments that offer 70% returns," sweet, grey-haired grandmothers would snap at financial seminars. After years of being faithful to those boring but safe GICs (Guaranteed Investment Certificates), they were ready to dump them and switch in a second.

They were getting caught up in one of the most explosive sectors of our economy, those sexy mutual funds and their steamy rates of return. Some of the returns, after all, were what we all fantasized about. Take Admax Global Health Sciences Fund. In 1995, it returned a whopping 66.3%. And what about Royal Precious Metals? A return of 63.8%. In the same year, Green Line Science and Technology returned 51.1%. AIC Advantage, 72.1%.

Top Performing Funds in 1996
(based on 1-year returns ending Dec. 31, 1996)

	% return
BPI Canadian Opportunities RSP Fund	89.1
Green Line Precious Metals Fun	70.1
AIC Advantage Fund	66.5
AIC Diversified Canada Fund	65.1
Global Strategy Gold Plus Fund	57.5
Bissett Small Cap Fund	51.0
BPI Canadian Small Companies Fund	50.5
Green Line Value Fund	48.3
Scotia Excelsior Precious Metals Fund	45.8
AltaFund Investment Corp	44.9

Note: Performance figures include reinvested dividends and management fees have been subtracted.

Meanwhile, those poor GICs, brutalized by 30-year low interest rates, were offering a mere pittance on our investments.

Unfortunately, some of these sweet ladies got caught up in the romance of mutual funds and didn't understand the returns aren't necessarily always that steamy.

What many of these ladies didn't understand is how mutual funds work, and how they allow investors to put money into an array of investments, from stocks, bonds, cash, gold, real estate, to commodities and even cash, which are held under one roof (the mutual fund).

The concept, dating back to the late 1800s, is brilliant and simple. A group of smaller investors pool their money and hand it over to a professional money manager. In return for a management fee of about 2%, the manager invests the money in a basket of 50 or more securities. By buying and selling at opportune times, the manager hopes to make capital gains, while collecting dividends and interest. The proceeds then go the investors, minus fees to cover management and administration. Returns will vary depending on what kind of mutual fund the investor chooses. They can also fluctuate, depending on market swings.

The truth is returns can be wild one year, then turn dull (just like a marriage) the next, even without a market swing.

What causes the perception of unbelievable returns is the time period mutual fund companies use to measure performance. For example, the AIC Advantage Fund, which returned a whopping 66.5% in 1996, returned a more believable 17% in a 10-year period from 1986 to 1996. Even its three-year return from 1994 to 1996 is 23.7%.

Performance numbers are affected by the fact that as of last October 1997, fund companies no longer had to factor in the October 1987 market crash when calculating 10-year compound annual returns. But now, returns will reflect the October 1997 crash.

In advertisements, fund managers cannot advertise returns that are more than 45 days old. And in their promotional material, returns no older than 90 days are allowed. The returns they boast must also look at one-year, three-year, five-year, and ten-year compound annual numbers.

Linda's Fund Tip

If you want to get a better picture of performance, check this out.

1. Look at how much money the mutual fund lost in any one-year period.
2. Look at how much it dropped in its worst down months.
3. Look at how long it took to get back into the black.

The best funds will be the ones that outperform others even in down days, or that recouped their losses quickly.

What many ladies also didn't understand was that the highest returns came from riskier mutual funds, which perhaps gambled on fledgling firms in a new explosive sector while money market mutual funds offer lower returns. These money market mutual funds are safe and liquid, and the kind of stuff the conservative investor may want in her portfolio.

Here's an example of some of the 1996 poor performers, many of which included less risky bond or money market funds:

Poor Performing Funds in 1996
(based on 1-year returns ending Dec. 31, 1996)

	% return
Scotia CanAm Income Fund	1.0
BPI Canadian Bond Fund	1.0
Retrocomm Growth Fund Inc	1.0
Working Ventures Canadian Fund	1.9
Fidelity RSP Global Bond Fund	2.2
Canada Trust International Bond Fund	2.7
Maritime Life Money Market Fund	3.2
Fidelity Canadian Short-term Asset Fund	3.4
Empire Money Market Fund	3.4
Manulife VistaFun Short Term Securities 2	3.5

The beauty of mutual funds is that you can pick the kind of affair you want, explosive, hot, and a little unpredictable, or steady, reliable and always there.

My mom and my mother-in-law are now among those sweet grandmothers who've made the plunge into mutual funds.

"I feel I am in more control, and I'm having fun with my investments," my mother-in-law cooed over the phone, while bragging about her new financial adviser, who had found her some good-performing international investments. Heading offshore for investment returns was something new for her.

In a nutshell, this 76-year-old dynamo, with her stunning Carol Channing appeal, is having fun playing the investment game. But she knows at her age not to take on too much risk. Her portfolio is well balanced with a bulk of assets in conservative investments.

THE MUTUAL FUND EXPLOSION

This is how explosive our love affair with mutual funds is. As of November 1, 1997, Canadians had socked an amazing $279.7 billion into these babies. Only six years before, on December 31, 1991, the total we had invested in mutual funds was $49.9 billion. Today, one of every three Canadians owns a mutual fund. Even during October 1997, the month our stock markets melted down, we were confident enough to invest another $4 billion.

"Investors stayed the course despite market turbulence," commented Tom Hockin, president and CEO of the Investment Funds Institute of Canada (IFIC).

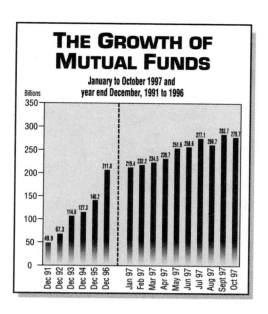

THE GROWTH OF MUTUAL FUNDS

January to October 1997 and
year end December, 1991 to 1996

Billions

HOW TO DIVERSIFY

Again, let me stress that the beauty of mutual funds is that they allow you to spread your money around—from the most conservative, like money market funds, to the riskiest, like equity-based mutual funds.

And they allow you to diversify your portfolio, which can help protect your assets through rough rides. For example, putting all your eggs in one basket that invests in equities can be tough stuff when a market crash hits. My advice is: never put all your eggs in one basket.

Some smart investors are putting money into what's called Balanced Funds, which offer a blend of investments tailored to one's risk tolerance. They can also diversify your investments by picking sectors that are expected to do well. Up to the year 2000 and beyond, analysts predict that banks and the financial services industry, as well as communications and media shares, will perform well. And they can diversify by taking your money to parts of the world eonomists may be predicting a good performance from. For example, Asia might be suffering now, but some analysts predict that by 2015, it will be booming again. The smart investor will buy in cheap and ride the wave up.

MARRY THE FUND MANAGER

Another beauty of mutual funds is marrying the fund manager. By that I mean you can get satisfaction knowing there's an astute manager, or a team of them, watching over your money.

Take Caldwell Mutual Funds, which boasts a group of eight seasoned, knowledgeable fund managers. They brag that a $100,000 investment in their Caldwell Associates Fund, made on October 31, 1992, grew to $225,786 by October 31, 1997, which includes the October 1997 stock market crash. That's a

23.34% return in the first year, a 16.35% return in the third, and 17.69% by the fifth year.

The trick here is to find the best fund manager who can predict economic trends and sectors that will do well, and who will act on them, not react. Also, it's best to seek out a fund manager whose style fits with your investment goals and philosophies, and who understands your diversification wants and needs.

For example, Caldwell prides itself on its more conservative strategy of investing in fixed income products or bonds, while seeking out value in large capitalization companies, including blue-chip firms, like Canada's banks, Alcan, Petro Canada, General Motors, and General Electric. Other fund companies may seek out value in riskier junior or small capitalization companies, or emerging growth markets.

The following will help you understand some of the different styles of fund managers and the different style of funds:

- **CAPITAL APPRECIATION FUNDS: These are controlled by fund managers who have leeway to buy any and all kinds of stocks and are not forced to adhere to any particular philosophy.**
- **VALUE FUNDS: With these, the fund manager invests in companies whose assets, not current earnings, are the main attraction.**
- **QUALITY GROWTH FUNDS: With these funds, the managers invest in medium-sized to large companies that are well established, expanding at a reasonable rate, and increasing their earnings 15% per year or better. This cuts out the cyclicals, the slower-growing blue chips, and the utilities.**
- **EMERGING GROWTH FUNDS. Here, the fund managers invest in small companies. These small-cap stocks lagged behind the market for several years and came into their own in 1991.**
- **SPECIAL SITUATION FUNDS. With these babies, the fund managers invest in stocks of companies that have nothing in particular in common, except that something unique has occurred to change their prospects.**

My advice is to read newspapers, surf the Internet, and listen to business reports. When you find that smart manager who is outperforming the rest, who has a track record of successes, then hook up with his or her fund.

KNOW THE RISK

The risk rule is simple. The higher the return, the bigger the risk. The following pyramid should help you understand what's the riskiest and what's the safest. Specialty or sector funds, whose returns can be steamy, are the riskiest. At the bottom of the pyramid are those safe money market mutual funds, which function much like a savings account. Money can be deposited or withdrawn at any time, without charge. You have access to your money at all times. But remember, if the fund is in your RRSP and you cash out, you'll pay the taxman.

CHOICE, CHOICE, AND MORE CHOICE

Mutual funds are like going on a dating game show. There's plenty of product to choose from. There are funds that invest in mortgages. Funds that invest in bonds. Funds that invest in real estate, technology, science, health care, and on, and on. There are also a host of new products aimed at satisfying the appetite of any investor.

A new kid on the block is Ethical Funds, perfect for the socially conscious woman who frowns on companies that are environmentally unfriendly, firms that may employ child labour, or cosmetic factories that test products on animals.

"When we first started in 1986, people in the industry laughed at us, saying it was a fad and wouldn't last," said Margaret Yee, vice-president of marketing for Ethical Funds, a family of eight funds worth $1.7 billion.

Yee explains, "First we look at the investment, then we make sure they are non-military, non-tobacco related and support child labour laws and safety laws."

Also getting a lot of attention these days are Index Funds, a mutual fund with a basket of investments tied to stock exchange indices. Indices used include the Toronto Stock Exchange (TSE) 300, which each day calculates the value of 300 stocks from three main sectors to decide how well, or poorly, the market performed. Other indices are the TSE 35, which lists the 35 largest industrial giants, and the TSE 100, which lists the next 100 biggest firms.

These funds can also be tied to the Dow Jones Survey of Industrials or the Standard & Poor's 500, which tracks the New York Stock Exchange, or the Russell 2000, which tracks relatively smaller American firms.

Here's an upside. Even though some may have exposure to offshore markets, some funds are considered 100% Canadian content, and therefore allow investors to park money outside the country without affecting their 20% foreign content limit.

Many funds are available, but some include Greenline's Canadian Index Fund, or CIBC's Canadian Index Fund. Also, the Toronto Stock Exchange offers TIPs (the Toronto Index Participation Unit), which is tied to the TSE 35, and HIPs, which is tied to the TSE 100. Index Funds are a more conservative choice than stocks or even mutual funds. But be careful. When the stock markets sag, so do these funds.

OH DARN, MY FUND'S NOT PERFORMING. SHOULD I SELL?

My friend, Liz, was in a tizzy at lunch. It was an unusually hot afternoon in May, thanks to El Niño, and though not yet summer, cafés had already opened their outdoor patios. We sat shaded from the hot sun, in a courtyard graced with blooming flowers and a bubbling fountain. "I don't know what to do," sighed Liz, a hard-working TV producer. "My baby just isn't performing."

My face flushed. Did I want to go there?

"What do you mean?" I hesitantly asked.

I could see this was important to Liz, as she confessed that in her forties, she was late tying the knot to any investment. "I spent my money on clothes, fun, and lunches like this," she sighed. "But last year, I finally did it. I bought my first mutual fund."

What was eating at Liz was that the returns were not as steamy as the salesperson had advertised to her. Not only had her mutual fund suffered through the meltdown of October 1997, but now the market, though scoring new record highs, was undergoing a series of mini crises.

As we sipped our wine in this downtown Toronto café, blocks away on Bay Street analysts were warning values could plunge anywhere from 10% to 15%. Even though Liz had made a wise choice by investing in a mutual fund mainly exposed to blue-chip shares, it was still hurting.

"Should I get out of this?" Liz wanted to know.

Like someone contemplating divorce, there are many questions you must ask first, I advised Liz.

Here's what Liz should ask before making her decision.

- Has the fund changed its management style? If not, maybe she shouldn't either.
- Does the fund have what it takes to become a good performer again? Some funds, for example, perform better in different markets, so know their personality.
- Are the reasons Liz bought this mutual fund still valid?
- Has she weighted risk and return? Her fund has minimal downside risk and good long-term growth potential, which suits Liz's style. Why dump it and maybe end up with a higher flyer that may look good now, but could cause Liz to lose sleep later?
- Would redemption fees eat into the profits she's already made?
- What is her investment time horizon? If she still has five, ten or more years to invest, switching now may be a short-term mistake with long-term consequences.
- Liz should ask herself if her portfolio has the right asset allocation between fixed-income and equity investments. Is she invested at home or offshore? Maybe instead of dumping this mutual fund, Liz should be looking at broadening her portfolio to ensure it's properly diversified.
- If Liz sells, will she trigger a capital gains or tax consequence? If her mutual fund is outside her RRSP, she'll definitely trigger a tax bill.
- Has Liz asked a professional adviser, one who's cares about her bottom line?

A LABOUR OF LOVE

Boy, did we love those Labour-Sponsored Investment Funds when they exploded onto the investment landscape, and that's because they offered tax savings so rich, it really didn't matter if they were poor performers.

Working Ventures Canadian Fund Inc., was the first on the street, and it invested money into fledgling firms. Then the labour-sponsored craze spilled over into sports, health care, entertainment, retail, and more.

What made these funds so attractive was the 20% tax credit the federal government gave to investors. Some provinces, like Ontario, matched the 20% tax credit, bringing the combined tax savings to 40%.

But the sweetest deal of all was when the fund was parked under an RRSP, the tax savings for a girl in a top income tax bracket could be as high as 93%. The only downside was that it's a riskier investment and the money had to be kept in for five years, or the tax credits were lost.

Then Ottawa tinkered. It cut the maximum you could put into these funds from $5,000 to $3,500, it cut the tax credit to 15%, and it ruled the money must remain in the fund for eight years. Still, that can be a total tax savings of $2,850 on a $3,500 investment, for an 81% return for a lady in the top income tax bracket. But these are risky funds, so be careful. Tax savings shouldn't be the only reason to invest.

WATCH OUT FOR FEES

Your mutual fund may actually be netting smaller returns for your retirement nest egg because of fees. Believe me, small differences in sales and management fees can mean big differences in the growth of your savings.

For example, a $10,000 investment over 20 years at an annual rate of 10% will net $67,275. But if management fees average 0.5% a year, the $67,275 falls to $61,416. Over 40 years, a nest egg of $452,593 will fall to $377,194, a 17% difference.

"It is important to know what you're paying when you buy a mutual fund, because loading fees and management expenses can make a big difference in the value of your investment in the long term," says Gale Caruso, president of Scudder Canada, a family of no-load funds introduced in 1995. Here's what to ask. Is the investment a load or no-load vehicle? Is there a deferred sales charge? Is there an administration cost to buy? Is there an early withdrawal penalty and what is the administration cost to sell? What is the management expense ratio (MER), which is what the fund manager will deduct annually? Toronto actuary Malcolm Hamilton warns that an annual MER of 2.1% will gobble up 39% of an RRSP over 25 years. Also, ask about the annual trailer fee commission.

Linda's Tip List for Buying Mutual Funds

- Make sure the fund salesperson promises to provide professional investment advice, and to diversify holdings.
- Make sure long-term efficient market strategies are in place.
- Understand that previous investment performance is no guarantee of future performance.
- Remember that the mutual fund is not insured by the Canada Deposit Insurance Corp.
- Make sure the fund manager provides audited administrative and tax accounting statements.
- Remember mutual fund performance is tied to market conditions, like:

  1. The state of Canadian and foreign stock markets
  2. Interest rates
  3. Currency values
  4. Political conditions (e.g., Quebec)
  5. Inflation

Like to sleep at nights and not worry about your investments? The answer may be bonds, which certainly become more attractive when stock markets get the flu, especially the Asian flu.

Bonds are great to add diversity to your portfolio. But don't expect the lofty double-digit returns of individual shares or equity-based mutual funds. Why? The value of bonds depends on a number of circumstances, and that includes economic conditions and where interest rates are heading.

Bonds shine during times of low inflation and low interest rates. That's why bonds did so well during most of the 1990s. As our country's central banker, Gordon Thiessen, governor of the Bank of Canada, let rates fall to 30-year lows to stimulate our recession-ravaged economy, the demand for bonds bearing higher rates of interest grew. And that pushed bond values up. In a strengthening economy when interest rates are heading higher, bond values will fall.

As I write this book, we're again watching rising interest rates, so we shouldn't be expecting a booming bond market. But if inflation remains low, even with some growth in the economy, and Thiessen doesn't panic and send interest rates through the roof, then bonds can still offer decent value.

Just remember, with bonds you're playing the yield curve game, and that can make any girl's hair stand on end. Bonds, though attractive, are complicated. They come with coupons, they come stripped of coupons (strip bonds), or forget the bond altogether and invest in just the coupon. Returns are based on yields, and if "normal" yields prevail, longer-term bonds are more attractive than short-term ones. Yet the longer to maturity, the higher the volatility.

There are government-issued bonds, with Government of Canada bonds taking the top spot as the hottest. There are corporate bonds, there are junk bonds, and there are convertible bonds that can be converted into common shares. All have one thing in common. The issuers are borrowing money, and bond rating agencies, like Standard & Poor's Corp., Moody's Investors Services, Dominion Bond Rating Service, and the Canadian Bond Rating Service, decide how much credit worthiness the issuers have by setting ratings. Big institutional investors, like pension funds and insurance companies, will buy bonds, but so too will investment dealers, who in turn sell them to you.

Here's how it works: Your broker buys your bond at a "bid" price, adds a mark-up, and then sells it to someone else at an "ask price." Commissions are built into the price. An alternative to becoming a bond expert is to stick to bond mutual funds, and let fund managers do the work for you. Here's how two popular bond mutual funds performed from 1987 to 1996. Note that 1994 was the only year with a negative return.

Bond Power
(yearly total returns)

	AGF Canadian Bond	Altamira Bond
1996	11.07%	8.97%
1995	20.61%	27.42%
1994	-8.47%	-8.84%
1993	19.62%	21.59%
1992	10.11%	12.37%
1991	20.44%	19.72%
1990	5.51%	7.44%
1989	12.16%	10.17%
1988	9.89%	8.83%

BONDS WITHOUT RISK: THE REAL WINNERS

Gotta love those government strip bonds that guarantee your return when they mature. How can they do it? The power of taxation. Unlike corporate strip bonds, which tie returns to a corporation's assets, governments simply rely on taxes to guarantee their returns.

That means you can buy a government bond and know when you cash out at maturity, your return is guaranteed. And unlike deposit-based investments covered by the Canada Deposit Insurance Corp., your investment is not subject to a $60,000 limit. Some of these bonds include Government of Canada bonds, provincial bonds, like Ontario Savings Bonds, and Ontario Hydro bonds. They're part of a process of financing government spending. They come in maturities from 6 months to 30 years and are completely liquid.

The Beauty of Government Strip Bonds

- You receive guaranteed re-investment rate protection and compounding of your money. Unlike locked-in investments, strip coupons can be sold before maturity.
- Bearer coupons are a direct obligation of the federal or provincial government, and are free of credit risk regardless of the quantity purchased.

WINNING BOND STRATEGIES

Linda Anne is 50. Financial planner Steven Pearl advises she should have 60% of her money in equities, and 40% in fixed income, like government strip bonds. But when Linda Anne gets closer to 65, Steven's advice is to have less of her money in equities and more in safer investments, like bonds.

A strategy to lessen the blow of fluctuating interest rates on bonds is to have a mix of long-term and short-term bonds, with maturities from 3 to 13 years. Steven warns that longer-term bonds can be more volatile investments because the longer to maturity, the more susceptible the bond is to interest rate swings. For example, if rates rise, the bond could be worth less. If you found yourself in a situation where you had to cash out before maturity, you could be forced to sell at a discount and lose money.

A trick some investors are using as I write this book is to buy a bond and wait for longer-term interest rates to fall. When they do, that's when they'll cash out the bond at a premium, and then invest the money into equities. The bet is by then the stock market will have hit bottom and be back on its way up.

But if you don't like to gamble, the beauty of bonds is that if you hold on to them to maturity, you are guaranteed the rate of return. For example, let's say a government bond offered in January 1997 cost $151.64 a coupon and is guaranteed to be worth $1,000 by its maturity on July 30, 2021. That means if you bought 450 coupons for $68,238, by 2021 you'd have $450,000 guaranteed. But while rates of return are guaranteed, like a GIC, these babies are totally liquid. In other words, you can sell at any time.

GICs: REAL DOGS OR NOT?

With interest rates near 30-year lows, even the most conservative woman investor lost her love for Guaranteed Investment Certificates (GICs), those investments with locked-in rates of return, which sell for $500 each at Canadian financial institutions. No wonder. Returns were cut in half at one point in the 1990s when the Bank of Canada rate hit a new low of 3.25%. Does that make these traditional investments real dogs?

Two bank economists crunched some numbers, and what they found may surprise you. In a nutshell, both a Bank of Montreal economist and a Royal Bank economist discovered that GIC returns are actually better in the 1990s than they were in the 1970s or the 1980s.

Why? "There's been a lot of talk about poor returns on GIC rates, but looking at historically posted rates is only half the picture," explained the Royal Bank economist. "We are actually better off on a real, after-tax basis with today's low interest rates, low inflation combination because the tax burden is higher when inflation and interest rates are higher."

Here's what they discovered. In real, after-tax terms, a five-year GIC in the 1990s returned 1.21%, based on a 50% marginal tax rate. That compares to the 1980s, when inflation once shot up 22%. Back then, that same GIC returned -0.89%. And in the 1970s, the return was -3.13%.

After-Tax Real GIC Rates			
	1970s	1980s	1990s
5-year GIC rate	9.07%	11.42%	7.72%
50% tax rate	50%	50%	50%
After-tax GIC	4.45%	5.71%	3.86%
Inflation rate	7.66%	6.60%	2.65%
REAL RATE	-3.13%	-0.89%	1.21%
30% tax rate	30%	30%	30%
After-tax GIC	6.35%	7.99%	5.4%
REAL RATE	-1.31%	1.39%	2.75%

The economist continued, "What many Canadians forget is that the high interest rates of the 1970s and 1980s were accompanied by very high inflation, which seriously eroded the purchasing power of the principal invested."

Linda's Tip
Look for the "Real" Rate. Real rates of return are key. Don't be fooled by the advertised rates of interest. Always factor in inflation and taxes in any investment you make.

NEW KIDS ON THE BLOCK
Something new on the market are index-linked GICs, which tie the investment to stock market performance. To the conservative investor, still shattered by the market meltdown, these may look attractive. But be careful. Yes, index-linked GICs can offer better returns than their conventional counterparts, but they guarantee only your principal, and most have some form of cap that limits earnings potential when markets heat up. In other words, they will do well when the market's on a roll, but if your money is in one when the market's underperforming, your rate of return could be 0%. Rules change from bank to bank, so read the fine print.

The federal government's Canada Investment and Savings, the arm of the Finance Department that manages Canada Savings Bonds, is also offering a new Canada RRSP Bond. Rates are guaranteed for up to 10 years. They're cashable and can be transferred each year on the anniversary date. As for good, old Canada Savings Bonds, in 1997 Canadians bought $6 billion worth of CSBs, but they're not as popular as they used to be.

The insurance industry, which lost market share as mutual funds exploded onto the scene, is fighting back. It's dusted itself off and revived an investment that could become a real winner as investors shun shattered stock markets. The industry's new darling is called Segregated Funds, and they offer the excitement of investing in Canada's mutual funds but with little or no risk. Segregated funds or "guaranteed investment funds" technically are insurance contracts or life insurers' version of mutual funds.

Under insurance law, they must guarantee to refund at least three-quarters of a buyer's investment upon maturity of the contract or death. But many insurers have boosted this guarantee to 100%. The mutual fund industry, though, argues that these guarantees are meaningless, since hardly any funds have lost money over 10 years. Segregated funds also offer protection from creditors in many ways and freedom from probate fees, which can cost thousands of dollars.

Advantages of Segregated Funds
- A guaranteed return of the original investment, but only on death or after 10 years.
- The ability to load up an RRSP with unlimited foreign content.
- Protection of the investment from creditors, and no probate fees on the investment if the holder dies.
- No transfer fees if the investor wants to switch among the funds.

MANAGING RISK: MAKING THE GIRLS FEEL COMFORTABLE
We girls generally don't feel comfortable with risk. Yet we know that without a little risk in our lives, attaining that dream of financial freedom is harder to do. So, how can we manage risk? The rules are simple: The closer we get to retirement and blue rinses, the less risk our money should be exposed to. But if we're young, go for it. Time is on our side. The bottom line is that everyone has a different risk tolerance, and it's up to you to pick the investments you're most comfortable with. Sometimes a balanced approach, a few eggs in each basket, is the best strategy. In other words, just as the pyramid chart showed us how

we can diversify our mutual funds, you can further diversify by adding other investments, like bonds, to your portfolio.

The risky stuff, with the steamy, explosive returns, includes:

- **Common stocks (also called shares or equities)**
- **Venture capital**
- **Limited partnerships**
- **Equity-based mutual funds.**

The following babies, though not as risky, still offer a little spice to life.

- **Bonds, like government strip bonds**
- **Preferred shares**
- **Mortgage-backed securities**
- **Mortgage mutual funds**
- **Income mutual funds**

If you like dull and safe, here they are:

- **Guaranteed Investment Certificates**
- **Canada Savings Bonds**
- **Term deposits**
- **Savings accounts**
- **Money Market Mutual Funds**

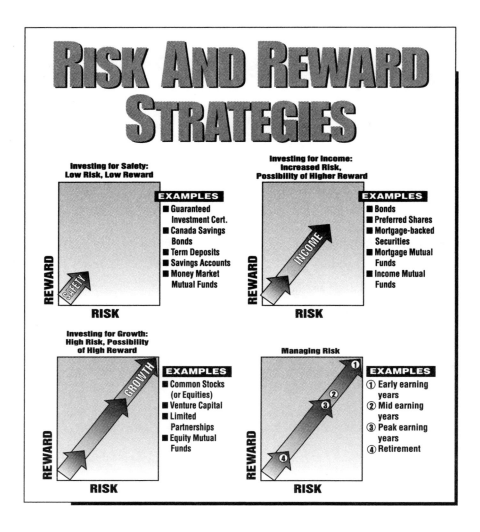

RISK AND REWARD STRATEGIES

Investing for Safety:
Low Risk, Low Reward

SAFETY

REWARD / RISK

EXAMPLES
- Guaranteed Investment Cert.
- Canada Savings Bonds
- Term Deposits
- Savings Accounts
- Money Market Mutual Funds

Investing for Income:
Increased Risk,
Possibility of Higher Reward

INCOME

REWARD / RISK

EXAMPLES
- Bonds
- Preferred Shares
- Mortgage-backed Securities
- Mortgage Mutual Funds
- Income Mutual Funds

Investing for Growth:
High Risk, Possibility
of High Reward

GROWTH

REWARD / RISK

EXAMPLES
- Common Stocks (or Equities)
- Venture Capital
- Limited Partnerships
- Equity Mutual Funds

Managing Risk

REWARD / RISK

EXAMPLES
① Early earning years
② Mid earning years
③ Peak earning years
④ Retirement

IS YOUR MONEY SAFE?

GICs, term deposits, savings accounts, and other bank deposit-type invest-ments, are guaranteed by the Canada Deposit Insurance Corp., up to $60,000 per institution.

For mutual funds, equities, and other investment products, there's the Canadian Investor Protection Fund, which will cover losses of up to $500,000 per investor, should a dealer or mutual fund company go belly up. This fund, which covers 194 member firms, includes all members of stock exchanges across the country, members of the Investment Dealers Association, and Toronto's futures market. Ontario, Nova Scotia, Quebec, and British Columbia also have provincial contingency funds to cover clients of independent mutu-al fund dealers. But remember, none of these funds cover bad investment decisions. In other words, if you were lulled into the greed of Bre-X or a bogus limited partnership, you're out of luck.

FINANCIAL PLANNERS: WHO IS A GIRL TO TRUST?

Finding that right financial planner is like finding the right man. Sometimes you never find him, sometimes he finds you. Sometimes you have to go out and go through several before Mr. Right comes along.

Of course, there are some girls who like calling their own financial shots and who don't really want or need a planner at all. Experts believe gut feel has a lot to do with whom you trust. It can also be his or her bedside manner. But word of mouth is always a good bet as a recommendation. For example, if you have a friend, an acquaintance, or an employer who's done well with his or her financial planner, check that planner out.

My friend Lynn faced this dilemma. A loving, single lady who's successfully climbed the corporate ladder at the *Sun* and is now in her forties, Lynn's become more aware that she has precious few years left to save for retirement. So she wants to get serious about it. One day Lynn left me a voice-mail message. "Linda, I don't know what to do. I've had a meeting with a financial adviser, but she just doesn't make me feel comfortable. She sent me my documentation, and there were errors in the numbers. Should I sign up with her?"

Lynn's lucky she had such intuition. Some people don't, and end up letting the wrong person take charge of their financial affairs, then part ways on bitter terms. I told Lynn to go with her gut, then I referred her to some advisers I trust and who've made their clients very happy.

Lynn met with them, and one of them, after sifting through her financial affairs, applauded her for taking control. His advice to Lynn, a recent first-time homebuyer, was to get rid of debt and try to top up her RRSPs, and use any tax refunds to pay down the mortgage. Feeling confident, and taking up the habit of reading any investment book she could get her hands on, Lynn, in the end, decided to go it alone, for now. "There may be a time when I feel I'll need someone," she said. Then she chuckled, "But I can always phone you."

If you do decide to tie the knot with a financial adviser, it's important to know what commissions and fees the planner will charge. And it's even better if he or she is a member of the Canadian Association of Financial Planners and follows the group's strict code of ethics and standards of practice. Remember what Ontario Securities Commissioner Glorianne Stromberg warns: Financial planning is basically an unregulated business. She also warns against the two evil twins, greed and fear. If a planner is trying to evoke these two emotions within you, walk away. Be realistic about the returns you expect. Yes, we've seen some real hot performers, but don't be blinded by the light.

Here's a quick checklist of questions you will need answered:

What about credentials?

Don't be shy. Ask the planner about professional accreditations and his or her membership in professional organizations.

What are they licensed to sell?

Different financial products require different provincial licences to sell. Anyone who sells a mutual fund, for example, must be licensed to do so. Stocks and bonds require a special licence. So do life insurance products.

How are they compensated?

Fee-only planners work for a flat fee or an hourly rate. Commission-based planners are paid by the companies whose products they sell. Some get money both ways. Some companies will offer additional incentives or bonuses. Make sure you're getting someone who's looking after your needs, not just his or her own.

Linda's Tip

Discuss These Important Issues with Your Financial Adviser

1. How much income will you need from a tax-sheltered savings plan? Do you have any special cash needs, for example, a new car or a holiday?
2. How important is it for you to minimize your future income tax burden?
3. How much flexibility in and control over your investments do you want?
4. How will you adjust your future retirement income for inflation?
5. How much income will your spouse or partner need if you die first?
6. How important is leaving an estate for your heirs or charities?

THE WEALTH LESSON

What have we learned so far? That to avoid poverty in our Golden Years, or even to reach millionaire status, we must first learn how to pay ourselves and stick to a plan. Starting early is bonus. And we must not be afraid of risk.

Linda's Wealth Creation Rules

1. Get rid of the notion that wealth is a bad thing. If you see yourself with money, you will have money.
2. You must learn how to pay yourself first—in other words, save. Shave a little off each paycheque. And learn how to live on less.
3. You must have a long-term plan, with a specific goal in mind. Without a map, you're like a boat riding the waves without a rudder, and you'll soon be sending for a life raft.
4. If you're sitting in a bar, enjoying a drink with a friend, grab a napkin and jot down your short-term, mid-term, and long-term goals for wealth accumulation. Even jot down career aspirations. If you see it, feel it, write it, live it, breathe it, it will happen.
5. Understand why you want wealth, and don't feel you have to make excuses to anyone for desiring it. Sure, money won't buy you love, but it certainly makes life easier.
6. Figure out what's best for you, and apply your investment strategy to it. Gut feeling is often the best feeling.
7. The best tool is education. Read books, surf the Net, and go to places you've never been before to find out which investments will make you money.
8. Study investment strategies to get you there, and remember the better the return, the riskier the investment. Go crazy when you're young, then fine-tune your risk tolerance as you get older.
9. Read about rich people. And learn where they like to invest.
10. As I've said before, if it's too good to be true, it ain't true. Walk away from get-rich-quick schemes, which line somebody else's pockets, not yours.
11. Never sock money into investments that keep you awake all night worrying.
12. Buy low, sell high. In other words, don't be afraid to buy when no one else is, and don't be afraid to hold on when everyone else is selling. Those who follow the flock end up a lamb chop.
13. Get rid of those two emotions, fear and greed. Those evil twins can bring you to the brink of ruin.
14. Don't be afraid to get started, no matter what age you are.
15. Don't forget to have fun, and laugh at your mistakes. Remember, nothing ventured, nothing gained—just like our quest to find the loves of our lives, as painful as it can be sometimes.

CHAPTER THREE

Why Girls Don't Want to Date the Taxman

Mom knew it wasn't just 30-year-low interest rates that were crucifying her household balance sheet. While her income stream was cut in half, thanks to these low interest rates, her tax load just kept going up and up. She wasn't alone in her frustration.

On a cold, blustery February night in the dead of winter, more than 6,000 angry families showed up at an anti-tax rally in Pickering, Ontario. One brave at-home mom underscored why so many Canadians were angry over the fastest growing personal tax load in the industrialized world. She came armed with a chart of her household budget, which was a fine illustration of why so many of us are finding it tough to save for our own retirement, why we're finding it tough to balance the household books, and why personal bankruptcies are so high.

Her husband, a unionized worker, earned a decent yearly salary of $42,383.52, which grossed $3,531.96 a month for the family to live on. But after all the deductions were taken off her husband's paycheque, including union dues, the family was left with only $1,512.54 a month. She then calculated the monthly household expenses, including municipal tax, mortgage, and services like home and auto insurance, which were now being hit with that dreaded 7% GST. The family's monthly expenses totalled $2,175.12. You guessed it. That left her family in the hole by $155.70 a month. What's so sick is that the total monthly tax grab was an unbelievable $1,374.99.

"We can't even pay the bills, let alone save for retirement," she sighed.

THE BIG TAX BITE

These numbers are based on an average Oshawa taxpayer's yearly earnings of $42,383.52:

Starting with a monthly gross pay of $3531.96 subtract ...

COMPULSORY DEDUCTIONS:

INCOME TAX	$1046.64
CPP	106.16
PSPF	223.54
UIC	89.40
UNION DUES	46.80

TOTAL: $1512.54

This leaves a monthly net pay of $2019.42
Next take out ...

HOUSEHOLD EXPENSES

MUNICIPAL TAX	$302.55
SHELTER COST MORTG.	1205.67
HYDRO H.& A.	170.96
PHONE	30.44
HOUSE INSURANCE	36.48
CAR INSURANCE	47.41
CABLE TV	25.93
WATER, SAN & SEWER	24.02
LIC. PLATE RENEWAL	7.91
FOOD & DRINK	323.75

TOTAL: $2175.12

IN THE HOLE — $155.70 a month

With the basic cost of living being $2175.12 a month, the average Oshawa taxpayer is left with a *deficit* of $155.70 to buy gas, clothes, car repairs, health needs, shoes, appliance repairs, entertainment, vacations, home maintenance, etc.

This tax rally was one of 22 held across the country in 1994 by the Canadian Taxpayers Federation, to bring home this message to federal Finance Minister Paul Martin: "No more taxes."

Earlier that same month, in the grand ballroom of the Sheraton Centre in downtown Toronto, I looked out over a sea of angry faces. These people had gathered for another rally to protest the tax spiral. The room was jammed, protest signs were everywhere, and emotions ran high.

On the stage with me that night were politicians of every political stripe, and they were about to get one hot earful.

"I'd give my mom and dad the money in my piggy bank to help pay the bills, but it's empty." This heart-wrenching testimony from a seven-year-old tore our hearts out. He and his family had travelled some 120 kilometres through a winter's storm to be with us. This event, like the other rallies, made national news. No longer could politicians and the media dismiss this grassroots movement as spoiled middle-class baby boomers who no longer wanted to pay their fair share of the tax burden.

The West Coast economic think tank, the Fraser Institute, crunched numbers to prove we were not moaning and groaning over nothing. In short, the average family of four earning $46,488 a year was paying out $21,228 in taxes. Even worse, $12,978 were indirect taxes, like the GST, which are paid for in dollars on which we've already paid income tax; the income tax load (which is among the highest in the industrialized world) was $8,250. Families were now paying more to the taxman than they were for clothing, food, and shelter. Never before has tax sheltering been so important in Canada.

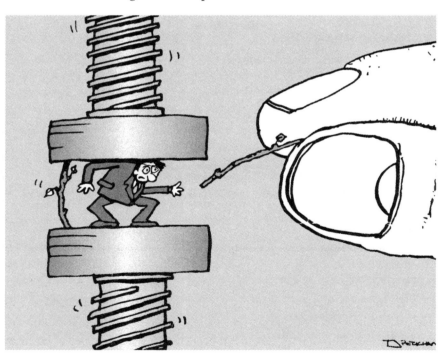

Taxes and Selected Expenditures of the Average Canadian Family Expressed as a Percentage of Total Tax Before Income Tax				
Year	Taxes	Selected expenditures		
		Shelter	Food	Clothing
1961	22.1%	12.9%	16.6%	5.7%
1969	27.5%	11.4%	14.4%	5.8%
1974	30.2%	11.0%	12.9%	4.9%
1976	27.3%	12.4%	13.0%	5.1%
1981	29.5%	12.0%	11.5%	3.9%
1985	31.9%	13.0%	10.5%	4.6%
1990	32.5%	11.9%	9.1%	3.6%
1992	32.1%	13.0%	9.4%	3.5%
1994	32.2%	13.0%	9.5%	3.5%
1996	31.6%	12.9%	9.7%	3.4%

WORKING FOR THE TAXMAN SIX MONTHS A YEAR

My cousin Trudy is the last person who wants a date with the Canadian tax-man. Why? Because this Canadian (and proud of it) from North Bay, Ontario, who married an American (the love of her life), has found why the land of stars and stripes can be so attractive. In her new home state of Ohio, she has to work only until May 3 to pay her tax bill, and then she gets to keep her hard-earned money. If she was to return to Canada—and believe me, she'd love to—she and her family would be working until June 29 to pay the taxman. That's when Tax Freedom Day falls. In 1961, it was May 3.

"We love Canada, but we just can't afford the taxes," sighs my American cousin, who works as a senior manager in a U.S. bank. Even when she and her husband factor in our universal health-care system, which would ease the burden of medical expenses for her handicapped child, it doesn't make sense.

A recent Price Waterhouse study underscores Trudy's dilemma. It showed that families living in major U.S. cities who were offered jobs in Toronto would have to be paid thousands more just to maintain the same lifestyle. For example, if Trudy and her family lived in Chicago, Illinois, and earned $100,000 a year, in order to enjoy the same lifestyle in Toronto, they'd need to be paid US$42,300 more just to pay the taxes.

RRSPs: The Last Place a Girl Can Hide

As the tax spiral grows and tax shelters are scaled back or eliminated, there are precious few places a girl can hide from the taxman in Canada. But there is one place. It's a safe haven called RRSPs (Registered Retirement Savings Plans). And if Linda, Erica, the tax-crusading at-home mom, or my cousin Trudy (if she dared to return to Canada) wanted to employ the best wealth-creating strategy, they'd use these sweethearts all they could.

RRSPs were born in 1956, but it wasn't until recent years, when Ottawa began warning us to save for our own retirement and not to expect government plans to be around, that they became widely popular.

How do they work? Simple.

They keep the taxman away from any gains made on investments while they're sheltered under an RRSP. In other words, our investments are allowed to grow tax-free unless we cash out, or until we turn age 69, when we must collapse our RRSP.

RRSPs also offer immediate income tax savings. Let's say my sister Karen earned $40,000 in 1997 and made a $2,000 RRSP contribution by the end of the February 1998 deadline. At tax time this spring, she'd get an $800 tax refund, if she was in a 40% tax bracket. If she was smart, she'd re-invest the tax savings or pay down debt.

In 1996 alone, Canadians socked $26 billion into RRSPs. That's up 13% from the $18.3 billion we contributed in 1995. But this is still a far cry from the $126.3 billion we were allowed to contribute. Why are we not maxing out? Simply because most of us can't afford to scrape together enough cash. That's because we'd need to earn $80,556 a year to make the maximum contribution.

The taxman, federal Finance Minister Paul Martin, knew that most Canadians couldn't find enough money to make the most of RRSPs, so despite our cries to leave our RRSPs alone, he scaled back contribution levels. For the 1998 tax year, we can contribute 18% of 1997 earned income, to a maximum of $13,500, minus any 1997 pension adjustment.

RRSP contribution limits

Year	Maximum Amount	Income Required
1998	$13,500	$75,000
1999	$13,500	$75,000
2000	$13,500	$75,000
2001	$13,500	$75,000
2002	$13,500	$75,000
2003	$13,500	$75,000
2004	$14,500	$80,556
2005	$15,500	$86,111
2006	indexed	indexed

- Based on 18% of cumulative "earned income" from 1990 less pension adjustments and contributions to RRSP after 1990.
- Earned income excludes investment income except for rental income.
- Carry-forward rules permit unused RRSP room to accumulate.
- When pension reform was first introduced in 1990, the $15,500 threshold was to be reached in 1995, which has now been delayed for 10 years. After 2005, the dollar limits are supposed to be indexed to increases in the average industrial wage.

Source: Marmer Penner

The hardest hit by these changes are upper income earners, like Christine, a broadcast superstar, who uses RRSPs to deflect the heavy tax load on her handsome six-digit annual salary.

But something the taxman did do, which the girls should love, is allow us to carry forward any unused contribution room in any year since 1991. This we can carry forward indefinitely. So if we net some of the $1 trillion in inheritances that our parents are passing on, we can use it as a wonderful way to keep the taxman away. But be careful. If you exceed your lifetime over-contribution limit of $2,000, you will face a tax penalty of 1% per month.

Getting into the Habit

A recent Royal Trust survey shows more and more Canadians are getting into the RRSP habit.

- In 1997, 48% planned to contribute, up from 34% in 1996.
- The average planned contribution was $4,283, up from $4,075 in 1996, or $4,049 in 1995.
- The average age at which Canadians are starting to make RRSP contributions is 32, which is a 12-year gap from the average age of 20 when Canadians begin working.
- Today's retired Canadians began making RRSP contributions at age 44.
- People from all age and income groups are using mutual funds rather than GICs or term deposits to invest for their retirement. In fact, in 1997, 65% favoured mutual funds, while only 16% preferred GICs or term deposits.

THE MAGIC OF RRSPs, RATES OF RETURN, AND YOUTH

For most girls, the only way to save the money needed for retirement is to put the investment under an RRSP tax shelter, and try to select investments that offer decent returns. For example, let's say Josie earns $55,000 a year, she's 40 years old, and she wants to retire at 65. If her investments yielded a 10% return and she let them grow tax-free under the RRSP tax shelter, she'd need to save only $2,012 a year to reach her goal. But outside an RRSP, she'd need to save $4,059 a year. Now, let's say her investments gave her a return of 12%. In the RRSP, she'd need to save only $1,281 a year. Outside, $3,031.

But what if she was only 30? At a 10% rate of return, she'd need to save only $1,189 a year if she put the money in an RRSP tax shelter. Outside, she have to sock away $3,421. At 12%, Josie would need to put only $645 a year in her RRSP, or $2,368 outside it.

Inside and Outside an RRSP

(Comparisons of a $2,500 investment at a marginal income tax rate of 50%, inside and outside an RRSP. The after-tax income is reinvested at an average annual rate of return of 8%.)

Years	Inside RRSP	Outside RRSP
5	$15,840	$14,082
10	$39,114	$31,216
15	$73,311	$52,061
20	$123,557	$77,423
25	$197,386	$109,279
30	$305,865	$145,821
35	$465,255	$191,496

WHAT'S ELIGIBLE, WHAT'S NOT

What qualifies for an RRSP shelter? Here's the list:

- Canadian cash
- Savings certificates
- Guaranteed Investment Certificates
- Treasury bills (T-bills)
- Mutual funds registered with Revenue Canada
- Government debt (bonds, debentures, notes issued by federal, provincial and municipal governments)
- Shares and debts of Canadian corporations listed on a stock exchange
- Stripped bonds
- Rights, warrants, or call options
- Shares listed on a prescribed stock exchange outside Canada

But remember, even though Canada represents only 3% of the world's investment opportunities, we're allowed to have only up to 20% of our RRSP holdings outside the country.

WHAT DOESN'T QUALIFY FOR AN RRSP TAX SHELTER

- Foreign cash, not even U.S. bucks
- Collectibles, like coins, art, stamps, antiques
- Gold and silver bars
- U.S. mutual funds, unless registered with Revenue Canada
- Real estate
- U.S. strip bonds

- Foreign stocks on exchanges that don't qualify
- Commodities, futures

Linda's Tips

Borrow To Invest

Let's say my sister Judi had $2,000 to invest in an RRSP, for a tax savings of $800 at a 40% marginal income tax rate. Let's say the investment yielded 7%. Her total benefit in one year would be $940.

But let's say she borrowed $3,000 from the trust company where hubby works to top up her RRSP investment to $5,000. At $5,000, her interest earned would be $350 at 7%, for a gross benefit, including the tax savings, of $2,350. Now, let's say she paid off the loan, at 9.5%, in one year. The total cost would be $143. That gives my sister a total benefit of $2,207.

Judi, do it!

Another tip: Most financial institutions offer RRSP loans at the prime lending rate.

DO IT REGULARLY

Another RRSP trick is not to wait until the contribution deadline at the end of February before you invest your money. The best tax savings come from contributing all year round. In other words, try making regular RRSP contributions. A neat trick is to time it when your paycheque hits the bank, by shaving off a regular amount and investing it.

For example, let's say Judi started contributing to her RRSP for the 1998 tax year on January 1, 1998, rather than waiting until March 1, 1999. And let's say she contributed $5,000. At a 10% return, over 30 years, she'd be $82,000 ahead, if every year she invested her $5,000 at the first of the year, rather than wait for the RRSP deadline.

SELF-DIRECTED: THE GOOD STUFF

A self-directed RRSP is just that. You—not a bank, not a mutual fund company—are in the driver's seat when it comes to your RRSP investments. And it means that whatever is eligible to invest in an RRSP, you can do it on your own. The beauty of a self-directed RRSP is that it's flexible and you're in control of the mix of your portfolio. A self-directed RRSP also lets you into the good stuff, like parking individual stocks and bonds in your portfolio.

You need only one self-directed plan, in which you can put all your investments under one roof. That way you keep the fees—which can range from $100 to $300—to a minimum. These fees were once tax-deductible, but no longer. So, to entice you to set up a self-directed plan, some firms are waiving fees. Shop around. You'll also pay fees when you transfer your investments into the self-directed plan.

Linda's Tip

Time Your Tax Savings

Another trick to maximize tax savings is delaying taking your RRSP tax deduction, if you think you're going to be in a higher income tax bracket next year.

Let's look at Mandi. In 1998, she decided to work part-time, which put her marginal income tax rate at 26%. In the same year, she invested $2,000 in her RRSP. If she took the deduction that year, she'd save $520 in taxes.

But she knew she would be going to a full-time job in 1999, which would put her in a 40% income tax bracket. By delaying the deduction for a year, her tax savings would grow to $800.

The same works for girls who are having babies. In the year they're on maternity leave, their income tax rate will fall. If you have to cash out your RRSP, do it when your income tax rate is the lowest.

REDUCE WITHHOLDING TAX

Sometimes we find ourselves in a situation where we need some extra money. As a last resort, we turn to our RRSP to "cash out." Try to cash out in amounts of $5,000 or less, because this limits the withholding tax you'll be forced to pay. For example, in most provinces, banks will withhold 10% on the first $5,000, 20% on amounts between $5,000 and $15,000, and 30% for anything higher than $15,000.

INVEST IN YOUR SPOUSE

Another trick is a spousal RRSP, and it can save big tax bucks, too. Let's look at Theresa, who's making good money as a marketing manager at a financial services group. Her husband, George, has decided to stay at home for now and be an at-home dad. A good plan is for Theresa to sock a few bucks, maybe $1,000 a year into George's RRSP. That way, she gets to deduct the $1,000 at her income tax bracket, but if they were forced to withdraw the money, the tax paid would be at George's lower income tax bracket.

Win, win? You betcha.

The only downside? Once Theresa gives that $1,000 to George, it's his, not hers. But in the event of divorce, the rules are that any gains in investments owned by both Theresa and George are equalized, then equally split. Even if George and Theresa were living together, they could set up a spousal RRSP. But if Theresa was co-habiting with a woman, she'd be out of luck.

NAME YOUR BETTER HALF YOUR BENEFICIARY

In a will (wills are covered in the next chapter), don't forget to name your spouse the beneficiary of your RRSP. That way, for example, if Theresa dies, her RRSP money can be transferred tax-free to George. But let's say she didn't have a will, or she forgot to name him as her beneficiary. At her death, her RRSP would be collapsed and the money included in her income would be taxed at her income tax rate. My advice: Don't let that taxman get his hands on any more money.

SPLIT YOUR INCOME, REDUCE YOUR TAX

Another strategy worth looking at is called income splitting. Let's visit Theresa and George again. Theresa earns $100,000 a year, while her at-home hubby, George, earns zip.

At 1997 tax rates, her income tax liability is $37,000, while George has no tax liability. Let's say Theresa could justify paying George a salary of $40,000. By doing that, Theresa reduces her tax liability to $18,100, while George now has a tax liability of about $10,000. By splitting the income, the family saves almost $9,000 on taxes.

TO RRSP OR NOT?

Sometimes there are more tax advantages to holding some investments outside your RRSP. Why? Because different investments are taxed differently. For example, equities are subject to capital gains, which means 75% of the gain on the investment will be taxed at your marginal income tax rate when you cash out. However, gains made on interest-bearing investments, like GICs, are taxed 100% at your marginal income tax rate, and you must report the gains yearly when you file income taxes.

Check it out. Crunch the numbers. Sometimes the tax savings can be greater by holding some investments, especially equities, outside an RRSP. Even if it's a mere 1%, over time, the savings will compound. And that could put a big chunk of change in your pocket, not the taxman's.

HOW THE TAXMAN HIT THE LAID-OFF

The numbers were staggering. In just one year, from December 1995 to December 1996, the number of people without jobs jumped from 1.45 million to 1.5 million. And that's exactly when the taxman slipped this by us: Federal Finance Minister Paul Martin quietly closed a loophole for people who had been laid off. It used to be that we were able to shelter our severance package from the taxman by being allowed to invest into a RRSP $2,000 for every year worked.

The loophole has been scrapped for any income earned in 1996 and beyond. But let's say Caroline is laid off after 21 years of service. She was earning $35,000 a year, and she was given a $40,000 severance package. Caroline decides to pay off her debts and take hubby and the kids to Florida, so she takes the $40,000 in cash. Immediately, there's a tax deduction of $8,080. So Caroline walks away with $31,920. But when she files her income tax, she finds the $40,000 has been added to her earned income, giving her total earnings of $75,000 for the year. Now she owes the taxman another $9,774.77.

As a result of her 21 years of service, she's able to transfer the entire $40,000 into her RRSP, without affecting her unused contribution room. So she fills out a TD2 form and gives it to her company. Now, instead of paying taxes, she gets a $6,060.02 tax refund, which, if she's smart, she'll reinvest in an RRSP. The bonus to this plan is that if Caroline doesn't find a job and is forced to cash out her RRSP savings, she'll be doing it at a lower income tax bracket.

A GREY POWER TAX REVOLT

The Canadians who are really getting hit by the taxman, though, are seniors, who are not only being forced to cash out their RRSPs earlier, but face a scaling back of government pension plans. It used to be we didn't have to cash out our RRSP until age 71. Now, we have to cash out or convert our nest egg into an annuity or Registered Retirement Income Fund (RRIF) by age 69.

For most seniors, like a wonderful nanny my family and friends affectionately call Mrs. Doubtfire, that means losing anywhere from $8,000 to $9,000 in tax savings. Mrs. Doubtfire turned 69 in 1997. That meant that by December 31, 1997, she was forced to collapse her RRSP. The biggest challenge she now faces is trying not to outlive her money. For example, there's a 54% chance she'll make it to age 85, a 31% chance to age 90, and a 12% chance to age 95. "That's probably a lot longer than she thought," comments financial planner Steven Pearl of C.M. Oliver Financial Planning. "Those who are healthy have an even better chance of reaching an advanced age."

Living Longer

	Age	Likelihood of Living Beyond			
	Now	80	85	90	95
Men	65	51%	30%	13%	4%
	70	70%	34%	15%	4%
Women	65	69%	50%	29%	12%
	70	74%	54%	31%	12%

Now that her RRSP had matured, Mrs. Doubtfire had these four choices:

1. Cash out the plan, and pay income tax on the full amount.
2. Use the RRSP money to buy an annuity.
3. Convert the RRSP to a Registered Retirement Income Fund.
4. Any combination of the above.

Here's what our sweet Mrs. Doubtfire had to decide:

1. How much income does she need from her tax-sheltered savings? Does she have any special cash requirements, like a new car, a vacation, a new roof?
2. How important is it to her to minimize future income tax?
3. How much flexibility and control does she want over her savings?
4. How much would her hubby need if she was to die first?
5. Does she want to leave anything for her children and/or relatives and friends?

WHY A REGISTERED RETIREMENT INCOME FUND

A Registered Retirement Income Fund (RRIF) really is an RRSP in reverse. A RRIF would allow Mrs. Doubtfire to still shelter her money from the taxman while withdrawing the amounts she needs. She's also still allowed to have up to 20% of her money in foreign investments.

A RRIF would also allow Mrs. Doubtfire to take her time making her investment decisions. For example, she could place her money in an interest-bearing money market fund and gradually move it to other funds that offer her higher returns. Another beauty of a RRIF is that if Mrs. Doubtfire was to die, and she had named her husband as the beneficiary, her account balance could be transferred tax-free to his RRSP or RRIF. The same tax-free rollover is available to a child or a grandchild. If Mrs. Doubtfire had no beneficiaries, the RRIF could be collapsed and the value added to her income and taxed at her income tax rate.

Minimum RRIF Withdrawal Rates

These rates are applied to the plan's value at January 1, even though the actual withdrawal doesn't have to be made until December 31.

Age at Jan. 1	Minimum Annual Withdrawal %
65[*]	4
66[*]	4.17
67[*]	4.35
68[*]	4.55
69[*]	4.76
70[*]	5
71	7.38
72	7.48
73	7.59
74	7.71
75	7.85
76	7.99
77	8.15
78	8.33
79	8.53
80	8.75
81	8.99
82	9.27
83	9.58
84	9.93
85	10.33
86	10.79
87	11.33
88	11.96
89	12.71
90	13.62
91	14.73
92	16.12
93	17.92
94+	20

[*] If under 71, your age at January 1 is subtracted from 90. Then that result is divided into 100.

Why an Annuity?

If Mrs. Doubtfire bought an annuity, she'd be handing over her money to a life insurance company or financial institution, which promises to pay a set amount periodically—usually monthly. The amount is based largely on interest rates at the time the annuity is purchased. Financial planner Steven warns, "This means that all future income from an annuity set up now could be locked in at today's low rates." He adds, "Think very carefully about your future needs; life annuity payments cannot be changed."

Here's why Mrs. Doubtfire may want an annuity:
- She wants a set level of income guaranteed for life or a fixed term.
- She doesn't want to make any ongoing investment decisions.
- She's not concerned about inflation.
- She doesn't need extra money for special purchases.
- She's not concerned about leaving an estate for her heirs.

Under the terms of an annuity, the only way she could leave anything for her heirs is if she's willing to accept less income to guarantee a set number of payments and she dies within a guarantee period, which is usually 10 years. After the guarantee period, any money in the account at death remains with the issuer of the annuity.

A fixed-term annuity, however, will pay Mrs. Doubtfire's estate the current value of all remaining payments. The newest kids on the block are indexed annuities that will increase payments every year. Check them out!

The Biggest Tax Grab Ever

It amazes me. After we've screamed and yelled over soaring taxation that's killing the family fabric in this country, we're lying down and rolling over for the biggest tax grab ever. This is the $11-billion tax grab Ottawa is hitting us with by hiking our Canada Pension Plan (CPP) premiums, while federal Members of Parliament still feast at the tax trough with their gold-plated pensions.

By year 2003, all working girls (and guys) will pay $48 billion more into the cash-strapped CPP. And don't rule out being forced to work to age 67 before we can collect, while our federal politicians can retire at age 55. Even scarier, there's still no guarantee the CPP will be around when many of us retire. Mom knew that. That's why she opted to take a scaled-backed CPP pension at age 60, rather than wait to reach 65. Meanwhile, here's how the working girls are getting stiffed. Let's say my sister Susan earns $35,800 a year. By 2003, the CPP premiums deducted from her paycheque will jump from $945 a year to $1,635. That's a 73% tax hike, as premium rates jump from 5.6% of insurable earnings to 9.9%. By 2030, they jump to 14%. Ouch.

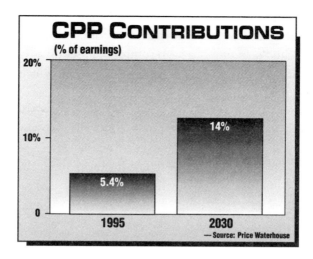

CPP CONTRIBUTIONS

(% of earnings)

1995	5.4%
2030	14%

— Source: Price Waterhouse

For the average worker, it's $3,100 more in tax in the next seven years. For the self-employed, who pay both the employer's and the employee's share, it's a double whammy.

Don't ever let Paul Martin tell you he's held the line on taxes.

What really hurts is that the majority of Canadians, forced to pay more and more into this pay-as-you-go-scheme, still have no confidence the plan will be around when they retire. In a recent Royal Trust survey, only 12% of Canadians said they were counting on CPP to provide most of their income when they retire.

Linda's Tax Tips

- Take advantage of every tax deduction and tax credit that's left.
- Learn how to take advantage of strategies that defer paying taxes, like RRSPs and pension plans.
- Learn the value of putting more money into the hands of family members with the lowest income tax rates.

Some other tax shelters still available include the following:

1. Hire your spouse or family members. For example, if hubby operates a business, either personal or through a corporation, he could hire you to provide services. The services must be necessary and the salary reasonable. You could also hire your children.
2. Give gifts to the kids, but invest in stocks, not GICs. Why? Because if you give your 10-year-old $5,000 in GICs, you will be taxed on the interest earned. But if you gave your 10-year-old $5,000 in stocks, and you sold

them for $10,000 a few years later, the capital gains are not considered yours. They're considered your 10-year-old's. But remember, that money is now your child's. In order to keep control of it, set up a trust account.

3. Benefits from life insurance or disability insurance, on which you paid the premiums, remain free of income tax.
4. Winnings from lotteries are also tax-free. But, believe me, you're much better off investing money regularly in an RRSP than blowing it on lottery tickets, where your chances of winning are remote.
5. Gifts and inheritances are also free of tax. It's the giver or the estate of the deceased who may end up paying tax, which of course lessens the amount available as legacies.

WE'RE WINNING THE FIGHT

Canadians like the angry Oshawa mother should take a bow. Slowly, we're winning the tax fight. Some provinces, like Ontario, have already cut income taxes by as much as 30%, while in Ottawa, the taxman—federal Finance Minister Paul Martin—is being pushed by economists, like CIBC Wood Gundy's Jeff Rubin, as well as the Organization for Economic Co-operation and Development (OECD), to do the same with federal income taxes. Why? Because these experts know we're killing Canada's golden goose with the fastest growing personal tax spiral in the industrialized world.

The numbers speak for themselves: From 1988 to 1991—when Canadians were hit with the hated federal GST—the highest federal income tax rate grew from 29.87% to 31.90%. Then it fell marginally to 31.75% to 31.32% to fulfil a promise by former Finance Minister Michael Wilson (father of the GST) to lower our income tax burden to lessen the pain of the GST. But at the same time, some provinces, like Ontario under NDP rule, were hiking income taxes.

In the end, income taxes hit new highs at the same time as we began paying for a GST with after-income tax dollars. We also became the only people in the world to suffer the burden of two sales tax regimes—one federal, one provincial (except in Alberta, where there is no sales tax). On the East Coast, the provincial sales taxes have been harmonized with the GST, a move that cost Canadian taxpayers across the country $1 billion in a federal subsidy.

Who knows? By the time you're holding this book in your hands, we may have harmonization across the land. But we may also have federal income tax cuts.

The fundamental truth is that our income tax burden is the highest in the industrialized world, at 14.5% of GDP (gross domestic product or economic growth), while in the United States (our largest trading partner) it's 10.1% of GDP. The average in the world's industrialized nations is 11.5%.

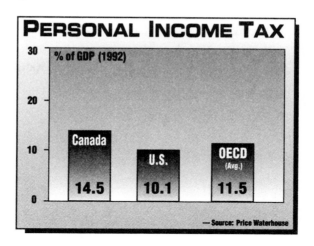

Our property tax load, which hits our homes and businesses, is also the highest. And so, the revolt continues.

But the good news is that as governments wean themselves from heavy debt loads, which in total are $1 trillion when liabilities like the CPP are added in, we need to borrow less from foreigners. And that means more wealth in the hands of Canadians.

More Tax Tips

If income taxes do fall, taking these tax deductions or credits before your tax burden falls may make sense. Every year, you're allowed to deduct these expenses:

- Tuition fees for yourself, or a student you're able to claim as a dependant
- Interest expenses to earn investment income
- Fees paid for advice for non-RRSP investments
- Spousal and/or child support, if it's set out in an agreement or order, dated before May 1997
- Child care expenses
- Employment expenses
- Safety deposit box fees
- Medical expenses that are not covered by a company-paid insurance plan
- Political contributions
- Charitable donations

And remember, if you do donate to a charity, consider gifting publicly traded shares that have appreciated in value, instead of giving cash or other property. Why? Because by giving securities as a gift to a charity, you cut the taxable capital gains in half, from 75% to 37.5%.

Another trick? If you happen to be an owner-manager of a closely held Canadian-controlled private corporation, declare a bonus to reduce corporate income to $200,000. This will reduce the company's taxable income to the amount eligible for the small business deduction. Check it out with your tax accountant or financial adviser.

CHAPTER FOUR

Estate Planning for the Girls: Protecting Your Assets

HE DIED AND DIDN'T LEAVE A WILL. NOW WHAT HAPPENS?

When my father passed away of a massive heart attack, my mother was left with two of her nine children still at home. For the youngest in the family, Tim—now a successful self-employed contractor—the blow hit hard. At the tender age of 16, Tim watched Dad die in his arms, as his heart failed at a sportsman's show in Orillia. Dad, a long-standing president of the Orillia Conservation Club, was host of that year's event. It blew our minds that this 49-year-old avid sportsman and entrepreneur extraordinaire, who had instilled in us a respect for the great outdoors and a love for small business, could be taken away from us so early in life.

At family get-togethers, tears still well in Tim's eyes as he recounts the pain of losing the father figure who was meant to guide him to manhood. Our second youngest sibling, Steven, also still feels the pain of losing his dad when still a teen. Despite this blow, he, like Tim and my other three brothers, have grown up to be fine, hard-working, successful men. Both Tim and Steve are still active in the conservation movement.

But for Mom, not only was this a heart-wrenching, emotional loss, but it was a financial one, too. Dad left an outdated, invalid will. And if there was a new one, no one could find it. And so, three weeks before my marriage to the Presbyterian minister's son, Dad's bank accounts were frozen, and I was soon to learn again that valuable lesson of budgeting and paying for my own way through life.

I paid for my own wedding, but the support from family and friends was incredible—especially from one dynamic real estate agent in town, Edith Page, my older sister's aunt through marriage. This now retired powerhouse who never married could move heaven and earth when she wanted to. And for me and my wedding, she did. And she did for any Tory whose campaign she worked on.

The rules vary from province to province when it comes to not leaving a will. In Ontario, the rules are simple. Toronto estate planning lawyer, Leslie S. Kotzer of Fish & Associates, explains, "The spouse takes the first $200,000 of the estate. And if anything is left over after that, the spouse takes one-third and the children split two-thirds." In British Columbia, the spouse gets the first $65,000 after all debts are paid, then shares the rest in varying amounts depending on how many children there are. In Prince Edward Island, the amount the spouse gets is $50,000.

WHO GETS WHAT IF THERE IS NO WILL

Name of Province	Amount of Preferential share (after debts paid)	Amount of Spouse and one child after preferential share	Amount of Spouse and two or more children after preferential share
British Columbia	$65,000.00	1/2 spouse 1/2 child	1/3 spouse 2/3 children
Alberta	$40,000.00	1/2 spouse 1/2 child	1/3 spouse 2/3 children
Saskatchewan	$100,000.00	1/2 spouse 1/2 child	1/3 spouse 2/3 children
Manitoba	$50,000.00	1/2 spouse 1/2 child	1/2 spouse 1/2 children
Ontario	$200,000.00	1/2 spouse 1/2 child	1/3 spouse 2/3 children
Quebec	0	1/2 spouse 1/2 child	1/3 spouse 2/3 children
New Brunswick	0	1/2 spouse 1/2 child	1/3 spouse 2/3 children
Prince Edward Island	$50,000.00	1/2 spouse 1/2 child	1/3 spouse 2/3 children
Nova Scotia	$50,000.00	1/2 spouse 1/2 child	1/3 spouse 2/3 children
Newfoundland	0	1/2 spouse 1/2 child	1/3 spouse 2/3 children

The pattern of decease is never predictable. Without a Will, you will be exposing your estate to the whims of fate. It is a common assumption that younger people will outlive the older generation, but consider the following:
• If you and your spouse are killed in a car accident your children will take your entire estate.

In my family's case, all of us willingly signed over our portion of the inheritance to Mom to ensure she could live in our family home and was able to survive. Luckily, there was only a very small mortgage on the home, which was easily paid off. And having been built to include an apartment, the family home was easily converted so it could provide an income stream for my mom. Mom would be okay.

Here's a further breakdown of who gets what, if there is no will.

> If there's no surviving spouse or children, the money goes to the closest next of kin, in this order:
>
> - Parents
> - Brothers or sisters (if they're not alive, but their children are, they'll share their parents' share)
> - Nephews or nieces
> - If no traceable kin, the government could get it all, depending on the province you live in

My family would have been spared this additional stress if we could have found the will. What's even harder on surviving spouses when there is no will is that they could be forced to post a bond just to be able to take over administration of the estate. In Ontario, that bond has to be equal to the amount of the estate. For example, if the estate's worth $500,000, the bond required must be worth $500,000. And if there are children under the age of 18, the surviving spouse may be forced to pay an annual premium.

Lawyer Les Kotzer points out that having a will becomes even more important for same-sex relationships or those living common-law. "If you're not married, the law doesn't guarantee an inheritance." That means if a partner in a same-sex or common-law relationship dies, the other may get nothing, even though the two have been living together for years.

If you're separated and you haven't changed your will, your estranged spouse may end up with the money, even though you don't want him to. Even just scratching out the ex-husband's name on the will may not work. "Unless a will is changed according to the formalities required by law, the changes may not be recognized," Les warns. "My advice is to consult an expert."

A will becomes even more important for couples with children. "Look what happens if both die in an accident," Les points out, adding there could be a court battle over who gets custody of the children. Even a single mother is wise to have a will, he says. "The single spouse will want to make sure the children are protected by assigning a guardian." But remember, anyone can contest that appointment. Under a will in Ontario, the appointed guardian has 90 days to file his wishes for custody. If there is no will and nobody applies for custody, the government can appoint a guardian and the children will inherit all the money by the age of majority, which in Ontario is 18. But with a will, parents can order the money to be put in a trust and set up the guidelines as to how the children will inherit the money and at what age. Here, Les advises the parents to appoint both an executor and a guardian, "one to watch over the children, and one to watch over the money. And make sure you pick people you can trust."

The cost of a will, on average, is $200, "which is money well spent," advises Les. But, he warns, keep the will current. "If you get married after you set up the will, it may be no good." Two witnesses are required for a will. But the provinces will allow what's called a holograph will, authored by the person and requiring no lawyers or witnesses.

Les's final piece of advice? "Be careful—your will is your final statement, and you're not going to be here to explain what you meant."

Linda's Tips for Wills

- Your will is your final statement of your wishes. Make sure it is worded properly and is valid.
- Review your will at least every two to three years, to ensure that new legislation or family circumstances have not changed it.
- Your will is private until the time of your death.
- As long as you're mentally competent, you can revise or revoke the terms of your will at any time.

POWERS OF ATTORNEY: POWERFUL STUFF

Mary learned the hard way about powers of attorney. She's a vibrant, former advertising executive who left her job to stay at home with her two children. Her husband, John, owned a successful trucking business. One steamy, sunny summer's afternoon, when they were driving home from their Georgian Bay cottage, fate hit. They were in a head-on car collision. John, who was driving, was air-lifted to the closest hospital, where he slipped into a coma.

Neither one of them had ever thought of a will, let alone powers of attorney. Mary didn't have signing authority for John's bank account. She didn't even know where his investments were, what bills needed to be paid, or what to do about running his business. Without a power of attorney, Mary found herself in a very uncomfortable position. She did not have control of John's finances. "I couldn't believe I had to put together a management plan to convince the government I was capable to manage John's financial affairs," sighed Mary, who, in order to take over, was also forced to pay a fee. All of this could have been avoided if Mary and John had filled out two simple forms, giving each other power of attorney over all their assets. This burning issue of making sure someone is appointed to take control is heating up as governments downsize and throw the responsibility for the sick and aged onto the backs of families.

Girls, face it: When it comes to looking after the elderly or the sick, the duties usually fall on the shoulders of women, who are the traditional caregivers. Just look at my friend Marie. Her mother-in-law, Granny, who hailed from Scotland, first moved in with the family in South Africa. Then, when the family escaped political unrest in the late 1980s and fled to Canada, Granny was to move, too. With a very small pension from the old country and no other income, Granny earned her keep by watching over the grandchildren and performing light household duties. But soon her abilities to do that diminished with old age. Walking was painful because her legs had become swollen as she aged, and it wasn't long before she was bed-ridden. Instead of Granny taking care of the kids, Marie ended up taking care of Granny. But Marie had a full-time job, and with some children off to university, who could no longer help out, it was becoming a strain. And so, finally, the day came when the family was forced to make the decision to put Granny into a senior's residence. Luckily, Granny kept her wits about her until just before her death and was able to manage her personal financial affairs. Her ashes are now in her homeland of Scotland. She was lucky to have her family behind her both emotionally and financially right to the end.

But many women aren't as lucky. And friends end up watching in horror as an aging woman can no longer make day-to-day decisions, as she allows unpaid bills to mount, as she no longer eats properly, and as her home becomes almost uninhabitable because the chores are no longer being done.

What if Granny hadn't had family to fall back on? How could she protect herself? Just like Mary and John, Granny should appoint a power of attorney. "A will takes effect at the moment of your death, but it does not protect you in the event of your becoming incapacitated by a car accident, a stroke, or just losing your mind," explains estate planning lawyer Les Kotzer.

And he warns that, without a power of attorney, "you face the potential of government getting involved and running your affairs." In most provinces across the country, there are two types of powers of attorney. The first is a "continuing power of attorney for property"—which would allow Granny to appoint somebody she trusts to handle her financial affairs and property. And it allows Granny to give specific directions, like consulting with a real estate professional before any real estate assets are sold. In short, this appointed person has the power to make any financial decision Granny is incapable of making—except her last will and testament.

The other power of attorney deals with personal care, under which Granny can assign somebody she trusts to take care of personal matters, like nutrition, residential care, medication, and consent for treatment. It may be the same person she trusts for her financial affairs. Or it may be someone different.

What happens to Granny if she loses her mind or health before she has appointed a power of attorney? Just as Mary found out the hard way, it would cost her time and money, explains lawyer Les. What happens here is that a capacity assessor would determine whether she was capable. "And if they found she wasn't, it triggers the government to get involved and maybe take over," he said. Worse, government will stay involved in Granny's affairs until somebody—a friend, relative, or acquaintance—makes a proper application to take over, and it's approved. Even if Granny has a hubby, there's no guarantee he'll gain control. "A sister, anybody, could try to fight the husband and win."

THE TRILLION-DOLLAR LOTTERY: HOW TO KEEP THE TAXMAN AWAY

It's like winning the lottery. Parents of aging baby boomers are starting to pass down $1 trillion of wealth they've accumulated. If you're a recipient, this is wonderful stuff. But don't be fooled into thinking the taxman isn't there trying to figure out how to get his grubby little fingers on the cash. "I'm so worried," sighed my retired neighbour Bobbie, a hot-looking lady in her sixties, who's been through two divorces and who, as an astute investor, has accumulated a fair bit of wealth. This lady has built up so much wealth, mainly through real estate, that when she did win a lottery, she took all her friends out for a night on the town they won't forget. Or should I say remember.

What Bobbie had in mind was to sell her home to her only child for $1, so if Ottawa decided to come after her home and to tax gains on her principal residence, her son would be protected.

"There's no doubt Canadians are becoming more and more worried that new inheritances taxes will soon be on the way," agrees tax expert Evelyn Jacks, president of The Jacks Institute. She adds that Ottawa understands that as our population ages and fewer of us are working, governments will be forced to rely less on employment for tax revenues, and more from taxing other income sources. The next new tax-grab target is the wealth Canadians have accumulated, such as pensions, real estate, and investments.

Right now, gains made on principal residences are tax-free. But gains made on investment properties or second residences, even cottages, are not. That's since the grubby taxman introduced capital gains taxes that apply not just to investment property, but also to an array of investments, including shares and mutual funds, if they're not held in an RRSP. Over the years, the rules on capital gains have changed, and, of course, with the changes, the taxman netted more, not less. It used to be that only 50% of a gain made on an investment was taxed at one's income tax rate, when cashed in or disposed of. Now, it's 75%.

Then the taxman scaled back a lifetime capital gains exemption from $500,000 to $100,000 and today it's zip. Only owners of small business corporations or farm properties, which qualify, still enjoy a lifetime $500,000 exemption.

"What Bobbie should know," says Evelyn, "is that by giving her son the home, she could potentially be creating a new tax liability for him." Why? Bobbie's son has already received the family farm from his grandmother for a mere $1, which is now his principal residence, and with the gift of his mother's home, he could end up paying tax on the gains of that residence, unless he moves in.

Children lucky enough to inherit the $1 trillion their parents have amassed will be well advised to invest the money in their RRSP, if they still have contribution room left. "It would be wise for them to maximize their RRSPs, and get immediate double-digit returns with their tax savings," says Evelyn.

How does the current system work? Let's say, Mom passes away, leaving a nest egg of $500,000, which includes equity in a home, money in a Registered Retirement Income Fund, a few GICs, and a life insurance policy.

First, her estate will pay no tax on the home if it is a principal residence. That's even if the home's been upgraded through renovations. But if it's a second residence, an investment property, or a cottage, it will be evaluated at fair market value, and any increase in value will be subject to capital gains.

But there is a way to defer tax on this asset. Her RRIF investment will also be valued at fair market value and added to her income at death, then taxed at her income tax rate. If she has a living spouse, or in some cases a disabled dependant, the money can be rolled into that person's RRSP or RRIF.

"What many single or widowed seniors don't understand is that RRIFs can push their income tax bracket into the highest level," explains Jacks. "This means leaving much less inheritance for their surviving family members. Receiving more RRIF money during a senior's lifetime, perhaps when they're at a lower income tax bracket, can be an effective strategy. If they don't need the money, they can gift it to family members directly."

Evelyn added, "I've seen seniors do without spending money on drugs, on things they really need, just because they think there'll be more money for their children. But the truth is, the taxman can end up getting half of your registered savings. Some estate planning can help."

As for GICs, those who inherit them will be responsible to report the interest at income tax time. Interest earned up to the date of death must be reported on the deceased's final tax return. Mom's mutual funds, on the other hand, will be disposed of at fair market value, and her final income tax filing will pay tax on the capital gains, if there were any.

Capital losses can reap tax benefits on the final return. There may also be other tax advantages if Mom was smart enough to make her capital gains election in 1994. For example, let's say Mom bought some of those nasty Bre-X shares. If she had unapplied losses that could be carried forward, she may be able to report the losses of her Bre-X shares at her death and reduce the amount of tax her estate will pay. "The mistake a lot of people make is not to report capital losses when they occur, not understanding they could be carried forward and used to reduce tax on future capital gains," says Evelyn. Besides Mom's principal residence, the only other asset not facing tax is life insurance policies, whose benefits are also received tax free by beneficiaries. But the time to buy life insurance is when you're healthy.

WHAT ABOUT THE FAMILY COTTAGE?

Theresa's lucky. The 43-year-old secretary and her husband, a TV cameraman, have enjoyed the family cottage for years with their two children. Theresa's parents, now retired, live year-round in a waterfront residence in southern Ontario and never use the beautiful family retreat, located in Ontario's upscale cottage country, Muskoka, known as the playground of the rich and famous. So, now at family get-togethers, the conversation for Theresa's parents and her sister often turns to how to pass the family cottage onto the kids without triggering any taxes.

Real estate lawyer Alan Silverstein explains that unlike principal residences, cottages are subject to capital gains taxes, so if Theresa's parents were to sell or even give the cottage to the kids, they would pay tax on any gains they made since January 1, 1972, to when they sold. That's because it was back in 1972, when Theresa was wearing bell bottoms and platform shoes, that the taxman decided to start taxing gains made on investments, including cottages. And, of course, over the years the tax rate has climbed. Today, it sits at 75% of the gain.

So if Theresa's parents were to sell her and her sister the cottage or even just pass it on as a gift, they'd pay tax at their marginal personal income tax rate on 75% of a $157,000 gain, since the cottage has appreciated in value from $53,000 in 1972 to $210,000 today.

One way to lessen the tax blow, advises Alan, is to include Theresa and her sister on the deed now, and therefore defer capital gains taxes by half. In other words, the cottage is now owned by Mom, Dad, Theresa, and her sister, as joint tenants. Another tax advantage, says Alan, is that by having joint tenancy, probate fees can be avoided when Theresa's parents pass on.

But here's another trick. Gains on principal residences are tax free, and Theresa's sister doesn't own a home. If the cottage is transferred to her, she may be able to use "principal residence exemption." If Theresa's parents don't want to give up control of the property, they could consider transferring the cottage into a trust, with Theresa and her sister named the beneficiaries. Check it out with an estate planning lawyer.

WHY ESTATE PLANNING?

- To make sure your money goes to ones you want
- To keep the taxman away, and keep government out of your affairs
- To ensure there's enough money for funerals, and to pay any taxes or liabilities
- To make sure the kids are looked after, both financially and emotionally
- To name a trusted executor, whether personal or corporate, to ensure your estate is administered properly

---

Linda's Tips on How to Select an Executor

- Pick someone who will act fairly and without prejudice towards those you've named as beneficiaries.
- Pick someone who's close by.
- Pick someone who has the time to dedicate to this task, and who's willing to do it.
- If the person dies or becomes incapacitated, make sure you pick a new executor.
- Pick someone who knows something about estate and trust laws, taxation issues, insurance, real estate, and investments.
- Or pick someone who's willing to learn.
- Pick someone with tough skin. With family affairs, there's usually the odd battle to two.

HOW TO CHOP PROBATE FEES

Probate fees are payable to the court or government in order to validate the will. Fees vary from province to province. Ontario charges the highest rate, at $5 per $1,000 for the first $50,000 and $15 per $1,000 after that, with no maximum. For a million-dollar estate, that could be up to $14,500 in fees. Quebec, on the other hand, charges no probate for notarial wills and a flat fee of $45 for English form wills. Here are some way you can keep the fees down:

- Make sure you name your spouse as beneficiary of any retirement income.
- Don't name your estate, but an adult, as beneficiary of life insurance policies or annuities.
- If you can, convert personal debt into corporate debt.

- Set up a living trust, so assets do not pass to your estate after death. When you die, those assets will be passed on to your beneficiaries as set out in the trust, not the will, which means no probate fees.

WHO PAYS FOR THE FUNERAL?

So, you've got a will and an executor, and powers of attorney are in place. But what about the funeral? Pre-arranging funerals can certainly ease the burden on family or friends. Many funeral homes are offering a plan to help you cover costs. It's called a Pre-Arranged Funeral Account, and it provides a tax-sheltered way to save for funeral expenses. You are allowed to put in up to $15,000 per person (or should I say body). The money is invested in an interest-bearing GIC and held in trust at your chosen funeral home. At death, there is no tax liability as long as the money is used for funeral expenses.

My advice: Sure, this means the funeral is paid for, but there are better ways to grow your money, like inside an RRSP and through more aggressive investments. This works for higher income earners, who are seeking more ways to shelter their money from the taxman. Benjamin Franklin was right. There are only two things certain in life: death and taxes.

TAXMAN GOES OFFSHORE

Mom has never run to a tax-sheltered tropical island to try to hide her money from the taxman. But if she had, the hiding would now be more difficult to do.

That's because strategies for taking our money out of the country have been clamped down on, after a rich Canadian family (rumours are it was the Bronfmans) were able to move $2 billion out of the country tax-free.

Now Paul Martin wants us to report all worldwide income and assets—a move that has riled rich Hong Kong families who fled to Canada's West Coast after Communist China took over the land lease. Martin originally planned this to take effect in 1997, but with complaints pouring in, it's now on hold. Still, sooner or later, we can expect to be forced to list all worldwide assets, when filling out our income tax forms, and that includes everything from a condo in the Caribbean to shares held in an offshore trust.

"The types of foreign investment Revenue Canada is on the lookout for are far from exotic," explains accountant Gary Dent, a tax partner with Doane Raymond in Toronto. "They include foreign bank accounts, real property, shares in foreign corporations and foreign bonds." Some of the hottest tax havens are the Turks and Caicos, Bahamas, Cayman Islands, Bermuda, and the United Kingdom's Channel Islands, where it's hard for Revenue Canada to ever track earned income in investments because governments in these places

don't tax income. Even Paul Martin has been accused of using this "dodge the taxman" gimmick, by registering his Canada Steamship Lines in an offshore tax haven. He vehemently denies the accusation.

Accountant Gary warns us not to be fooled into thinking this is just a clampdown on the idle rich. He says the taxman wants to know about all foreign investments and assets worth $100,000 or more and explains it's easy to hit this threshold. "It doesn't take much to reach $100,000 when you take into account the foreign exchange rate," warns Gary. "Foreign rental property and shares in a U.S.-based corporation listed on the New York Stock Exchange, combined with deposits in U.S. banks accounts, can bring you over the limit in no time."

Offshore Taxman

If you think the new foreign reporting rules are only for the upper crust, think again. Here's all it would take to put you over the $100,000 threshold.

Your Property	Your Cost
U.S. rental condo	$ 84,000 Cdn.
Shares listed on NYSE	$ 16,800
On deposit in U.S. bank	$ 4,200
TOTAL VALUE OF U.S. ASSETS	$105,000

Gary points out that the new rules don't apply to properties for personal use like a vacation and that are not rented out, or to property in an active business, holdings in certain foreign mutual funds, and foreign holdings in an RRSP or RRIF.

Under the old rules, Canadians were responsible only for reporting earned income outside Canada and paying tax on it, not listing assets. This means if Mom owned a condo in Florida and rented it out, she could soon be tracked by Revenue Canada to make sure she's reporting the income earned from the rental.

"Stiff penalties await those who fail to comply with the new rules to report foreign holdings," warns Gary.

If you refuse to fill out the new form and you knowingly have assets abroad, you could face penalties as high as $1,000 a month for up to two years.

Ottawa is also clamping down on those who earn worldwide income and refuse to report it. These fines range from $100 to $12,000 a month, with additional penalties up to 10% of the value of the foreign property. To stop money from fleeing the country, Ottawa has also introduced a new withholding tax for family trusts transferred out of Canada.

The lesson? Every move you make, every breath you take, the taxman is watching.

Linda's Estate Planning To-Do List

- Make sure you have a valid up-to-date will.
- Make sure you have a power of attorney, one for your financial affairs, and one for your personal care.
- Toughen your will to lessen the blow of probate fees.
- Check out family trusts, and see if they work for you.
- Have a record of all your personal affairs.
- Review your life insurance.
- Pre-plan your funeral.

SAFE HAVEN FOR SNOWBIRDS

Erica's grandmother can't wait for Christmas to be over. Every year, on Boxing Day, this bustling 67-year-old widow packs up her summer clothes, buys an airline ticket, and flies to sunny Florida, where she'll spend four glorious, snowless months playing cribbage and walking the beaches with her girlfriends.

Granny loves her Clearwater beach condo. And she loves her silver 1989 convertible. Not one spot of rust, and only 40,000 kilometres on it, it takes her where she needs to go, which is usually a quick visit to the bank to get some U.S. funds from her account for a shopping spree or two.

Life is grand. But what would happen if one day Granny was in a car accident? And she ended up in hospital in a coma? "Even if she appointed a power of attorney in Canada to manage her affairs, she's in trouble," explains estate planning lawyer Barry Fish of Fish & Associates in Thornhill, Ontario. That's because her Canadian-appointed power of attorney has no power under Florida law and won't be recognized by the state's registry system or its financial institutions. "She must appoint a durable power of attorney in Florida," says Barry. "Without it, she may need a court order to establish authority." Under Florida law, a durable power of attorney covers both financial and health-care matters. In Canada, though, most provinces separate the two. When it comes to Granny's Canadian will, her Florida assets are safe and sound within it, says Barry. But he still advises that she get advice from a Florida lawyer to ensure all her assets are protected.

Now, here's a trick. If Granny was to get a separate Florida will, she could save on probate fees. That's because with just a Canadian will, her Florida assets will be added in, and the probate fees set accordingly. But if she gets a Florida will, she must be careful to instruct the lawyer to ensure her Canadian will is still valid. The same applies to appointing a Florida power of attorney. Make sure the Canadian power of attorney is still valid.

WHY LIFE INSURANCE?

Simply put, life insurance will protect your family if you were to die tomorrow.

You need enough to cover all your debts, like mortgages, car loans, lines of credit, etc. You may also want to cover your funeral costs, university education, and child care, if there is any.

The rule of thumb is that the younger you are, the more coverage you need.

WHOLE LIFE VERSUS TERM

Most financial experts will argue that term insurance—a simple, low-cost insurance—is the way to go. It works like car or home insurance. You pay a premium for the protection, and nothing else.

Whole-life products, though, promise to pay you a fixed amount on death; this is called the "face value" of the plan. It also offers an investment or "cash value." The downside here is that if you were to die, your spouse gets only the face value.

Many will argue it's better to take out term insurance to protect yourself, and invest the difference in your own investment portfolio.

You can take out life insurance on your mortgage or other loans, but experts argue it's less expensive just to top up your own term life insurance policy than to buy additional life insurance. And don't forget to check out how much insurance coverage you may already have, thanks to your employer.

When it comes to life insurance on mortgages, the stories can be horrendous. Take Annette, a hard-working house cleaner who moved to Canada from Portugal to give her family a better life. She and her husband scrimped and saved and finally bought a home. They also took out joint life insurance with their mortgage at their bank. Premiums were being deducted every month, which led Annette to believe all was fine—until her husband became ill, was hospitalized, and later passed away.

When she showed up at her bank with the insurance forms, hopeful that insurance would pay what was left owing on the house, she was told her husband had been rejected for coverage. She persisted, showing bank statements on which premiums had been deducted monthly, but bank staff said the premiums were taken in error and offered a refund.

Angry and feeling betrayed, she hired a lawyer. But a year later, the case was still not settled—and she can barely afford to keep up with the mortgage bills, after being handed a $25,000 legal bill. A close friend confided, "For a year, she has struggled to cope with the increasing stress caused by the loss of her husband, the cruel and callous actions of the banking and legal machinery, and the ongoing burden of supporting her household, including still paying for a funeral on a monthly payment plan." The advice here is to watch for weasel clauses. Always read the fine print. And ask your bank to give you a copy of the insurance document to ensure you are truly covered. If your husband takes control of such matters, ask him to open the files and go over details with you. Like Annette, you may face life alone and be left with the financial consequences.

CHAPTER FIVE

Family Finances I: Divorce and How the Buck Can Break Up a Home

THAT JERK: HE DIVORCED ME

The numbers make us wonder why we ever walk down the aisle. Anywhere from 35% to 50% of marriages in Canada will end in divorce. And the chances of a bitter end to a relationship sealed in the vows of matrimony are greater if you live in an urban area.

My lovable, foxy Aunt Gale knows this well. Her first marriage to the man of her dreams ended in divorce. She walked away with her prized sports car, and they split the assets. Not only did she suffer the emotional blows, but financially it was also devastating. "You never realize the standard of living you're enjoying until you lose it," she sighed, after leaving her meticulously furnished four-bedroom home, full of antiques and heirlooms, and moving to a two-bedroom apartment. Also gone were the wonderful treks south that she had enjoyed with her ex, who as a top salesman was rewarded by his firm with holidays away.

Years passed before my aunt met another man and married. But this relationship, too, didn't last, and as I write this, my aunt is still embroiled in a bitter battle over the $30,000 of inheritance she brought to the table when she tied the knot for the second time. There are also disputes over any equity that she may have in their matrimonial home that they had renovated in a quaint village in rural Ontario. The plan had been to renovate, sell, and make some cash.

Rules of splitting assets when a divorce hits are pretty simple, explains one of Canada's leading family law lawyers, Stephen Grant of Toronto law firm Gowling, Strathy & Henderson. "Property laws vary from province to province, but generally parties share equally the assets acquired after marriage, except inheritances and/or gifts," states Grant.

Let's say Aunt Gale's $30,000 inheritance grew to $50,000 during the time she was married. Under what is called "equalization of net family property," she would have to share the $20,000 gain with her ex, unless she invested it in an investment that offers capital gains. She does not have to share the original $30,000 inheritance.

But here's where her $30,000 really went. A total of $15,000 was invested in the home, which they owned jointly. And, unfortunately, the value of that home fell as deflation hit our housing sector for the first time in post-war history. The other $15,000 went to buy a car for her ex, which he claimed he so badly needed. "She may have to kiss the money goodbye," comments my tax accountant, Steve Ranot, a partner with Marmer Penner, a Toronto-based accounting firm that specializes in business valuation and litigation accounting. Steve is a *Toronto Sun* tax columnist, whose humorous wit at my financial seminars is widely popular. But when it comes to the cases of divorce, he'll comment that there is little to laugh about.

Like my aunt's case, which will lead to divorce. My aunt first paid $1,000 to a lawyer to help her set up a separation agreement and get some of her money back. In the end, nothing happened. It wasn't until she dealt with a real estate lawyer, who helped her in the sale of the matrimonial home, that she received some help.

She has now settled that $20,000 is her inheritance, giving up $10,000. And through a promissory note, she's been able to be guaranteed that any proceeds from the sale of the home, up to $20,000, will be hers. Time will tell if she ever gets her money.

This marriage has been one of the toughest lessons of her life. "I thought this marriage would benefit both of us, and in the end I've paid dearly," she said. Will she ever re-marry? "I think it would be very difficult to trust a man again." What worries her is that she's now in her fifties, all her assets, including a lakeside condo she once owned, are gone. And she has no retirement nest egg to fall back on, at all. In fact, she's even had to resort to social assistance just to get by. "After taking care of myself for so long, and paying my own way, I'm basically a poor person," she sighed. "And when it comes to fighting back, a lawyer can cost $165 an hour or more. What woman can afford that?"

Here's what every woman should know, as tax accountant Steve Ranot explains: "Each spouse is entitled to an equalization of the net family property." So, what is net family property? "It's really the increase in net worth of each spouse during marriage."

Here's how it works: Mary and Fred tie the knot on June 2, 1978, and both come to the marriage with no assets. By 1997, Fred's personal net worth, including collectibles, RRSPs, company pension, a Jag, grows to $350,000.

Mary's net worth grows to $280,000. When they split on July 3, 1997—some 19 years after walking down the aisle together—Fred owes Mary a lump-sum equalization payment of $35,000. That's one-half the value of Fred's growth in their net family property. As a result, each ends up with $315,000.

As well, because Fred earns a larger annual income than Mary, she can make a claim for support payments. "As long as she can prove the need for the money, and he has the ability to pay, she'll get support," says Steve. If Mary earned the higher income, Fred could ask for support.

The only asset treated differently, says Steve, is the matrimonial home. If purchased together during marriage, the rules are simple. It will be included in the equalization process, and they'll share in the growth of the value. But let's say Mary owned the home mortgage-free when she married Fred. And let's say the three-bedroom suburban ranch home was worth $68,000 back then. But today, even after its value hit $260,000 in 1989 then fell to $230,000 in 1997 as deflation struck, it still gained $162,000 in worth. Poor Mary will have to share the whole $230,000 with Fred, and kiss her original $68,000 goodbye.

Steve's advice is this: if you do inherit money or receive a gift, and your marriage is on rocky grounds, don't be a fool. "If you blow it on a vacation, pay down the mortgage on your jointly owned home, or buy your kid a horse, it's gone," he says. Even if you invest it in interest-bearing vehicles, like Canada Savings Bonds, you can get back only the original inheritance and you have to share the compound growth of the investment. But if you invest in an investment that offers capital gains, like an equity mutual fund, then the money is all yours. The bottom line: Protect your assets.

PRENUPTIALS: DO THEY WORK?

Billionaire Bill Gates did it. The popular single rich man, who made his fortune with Microsoft and dashed many a woman's hope of marrying rich by landing him, tied the knot with somebody else. But before this computer wizard walked down the aisle with Melinda, he made sure his bride signed a prenuptial agreement. When boiled down, his new wife will inherit only $1 billion (don't we feel sorry for her) if billionaire Bill should pass away—while the lion's share of his $40 billion in assets will go to charity.

But here's the weird part of Gates's agreement. His new wife also agreed to allow him to spend an annual holiday with his former girlfriend, venture capitalist Ann—who back in 1976 started up her own software company with a $1,000 loan from her brother. Today, her firm is worth some $200 million and growing. Apparently, the two former love birds spend their holiday at her cottage in North Carolina, playing golf, walking on the beach, hang-gliding, and talking about biotechnology. Comments Steve Ranot: "Prenuptial agreements can be a smart thing to do, but rules vary." Check it out with a family law lawyer.

LEATHERDALE NAME MAKES HISTORY

I first met Doug Leatherdale in 1992. He had seen my name in the pages of the *Toronto Sun* and was curious about it, so he called to arrange a meeting.

"Who's your dad?" he asked. I recited the family tree—my dad was Bruce Leatherdale, his dad was Gordon, and his grandfather was Adrian. I explained how his great-grandfather, Elias, had migrated from a tiny hamlet in England and settled in the rolling hills of Medonte Township, near Coldwater, Ontario.

Doug visited me at the *Sun*, and I was stunned by how similar his looks were to my own father's. We figured out that Doug was my dad's second cousin. The blond hair, the striking blue eyes, the six-foot-plus stature, and the big hands, all showed there were strong genes in this Leatherdale family. We played with the idea that there was definitely Viking blood in our ancestry. I was impressed and felt a little nostalgic when he commented how I looked like his little sister, who had passed away. It wasn't until the end of the tour of the *Toronto Sun* that he quipped, "You know, my name's been in newspapers, too."

Curious, I ventured into our library after Doug left. There it was in black and white. Doug's bitter divorce in 1980 from his first wife, Barbara, made it all the way to the Supreme Court of Canada in Ottawa. At the heart of the battle were non-family assets, like $40,000 that was sitting in his retirement nest egg. The money included Bell Canada stock and a Registered Retirement Savings Plan through Bell Canada, where he had worked as a supervisor.

After the 19-year marriage ended in divorce, Barbara had already been awarded half the family assets, as well as the house. She also went after child support and was awarded $700-a-month support for herself and her teenaged son. The original ruling also said Barbara could have half of the $40,000 retirement nest egg, but then an Ontario Court of Appeal ruled she was not entitled to share in the investments. That's when she took the fight to the Supreme Court of Canada and eventually won. In the end, she got $10,000 of Doug's $40,000 in retirement money. So now company pension plans, which used to be shielded from divorce, are fair game.

When I called Doug to discuss it, he was still bitter and angry even though more than 10 years had passed. And he vowed he'd never re-marry. Just to let you know, I called him up last summer to ask him to attend our family reunion. Guess what? His new wife answered the phone.

Guess it's true—love rules.

ANOTHER COURT CASE

The next Supreme Court case dealing with divorce to make national news was one involving Quebec social worker Suzanne Thibaudeau, who was angry that she had to pay income tax on the $1,150 a month she received in child support payments, while her ex-husband did not. In the end, Suzanne won the battle, and effective May 1, 1997, any new child support agreements entered into would have to follow these new tax rules: No longer would the recipient of child support payments (usually women) have to pay income tax on the money received. And no longer would the payer (usually a man) be allowed to claim child support payments as a tax deduction. Some 317,000 single mothers across the country, like my younger sister Karen, rallied together with a victory cry. They would receive some $330 million in tax refunds. But did they really win?

"Revenue Canada finally said, okay, Suzanne, if you want to complain about his tax deduction, we'll take it away and we'll laugh all the way to the bank," comments Steve Ranot. Why does he say this? Because Revenue Canada just gained a $400-million-a-year windfall. The reason is that those who pay child support (usually men) are normally in a higher tax bracket, while the recipients of child support (usually women) are in a lower one. By reversing the tax rules, Revenue Canada gets more money—and families get less.

For the payer, usually the divorced male, it's a win-win situation. All he has to do is make a court application to pay less money now that he's no longer able to deduct the payment on income taxes.

All child support payment agreements dated after May 1, 1997, must adhere to the new federal rules. Provinces have also set up new guidelines for child support payments. If the parents disagree on what is to be paid, they can take the issue to court, and in the end the guidelines will rule.

What's unfair and inequitable about this new system is that it does not take into consideration the income the custodial parent earns. Let's say a husband and wife split. The husband earns $50,000 a year, and the wife earns $100,000, and she gets custody of the kids. Despite the fact the wife earns twice the amount of her ex, he still has to pay $687 a month in support payments, if they reside in Ontario and abide by the Family Law Act. (Each province sets out its own amount in its guidelines.) Even if he's collecting employment insurance, he'll have to pay something. "Basically, this is an inequity in the system," explains Steve. "But in the interest of simplicity, governments drafted the guidelines like this."

Provinces are also getting tougher with dead-beat dads, who don't pay— but still the horror stories abound. Like a friend of mine, who called and pleaded, could I help his little sister? After 10 years of marriage, three children, and many a beating, the jerk finally left her high and dry. When it came to child support, he just wasn't paying. His excuse? Money was tight even though he and his new girlfriend were driving around in a brand-new car, and he'd started up a new firm. Then there's another friend who's angry there is no accountability as to how his child support payments are spent. "I pay good money, yet my little girl is wearing a second-hand winter coat," he sniffed. "And my ex just spent $7,000 on a facelift."

But some women see divorce differently. Take Sandy, an attractive, blonde bartender. "I walked away and left my two children." Her confession stunned me. How can anyone leave their children? "My husband earns a lot more money than I do. We had a beautiful home. Why should I drag my children away from that lifestyle and force them to live on assistance in an apartment?" she explained.

She moved out, but every morning reported to the family home at 7 a.m. to make the children breakfast, make lunch, and send them off to school. She wanted no support, no share of the assets, just her peace of mind, and to see her children. "It was, after all, my decision to leave. I knew we could work it out."

In the end, there was no custody battle. She and her husband shared custody. There was also no fight over support payments. Just a routine in which they shared the responsibilities and tried to get along and get on with their lives. Today, the children are 17 and 14, and they spend equal time with each parent.

Linda's Tip
Chill Out
Any angry woman who cries out, "I'll take you to the cleaners, and you'll never see your kids again" is being greedy and is thinking of her own best interests, not the children or her spouse.
Sure, breakups are bitter. And it hurts like hell. But when cooler heads prevail, as the Beatles' hit goes, "We Can Work It Out."

HOW THE MIGHTY BUCK CAN BREAK UP A HOME

Did you know we'll spend more time planning a wedding and a honeymoon than we ever will on our personal finances? Yet when it comes to marriage breakups, it's often money that is the root of all evil. That, or an infidelity.

The bottom line is that boys and girls view money management differently, and usually someone is made to feel guilty or inadequate when it comes to the mighty buck.

There's the money martyr who won't spend anything on herself and nags her spouse to get out there and earn more because "our kids need designer jeans" or "our daughter needs a horse with a stable, riding lessons, the works." Or there's the chauvinistic male: "Don't worry your pretty little head about it." Or the free-spending partner, who buys compulsively, hides the bills, lies about what is owed, and lashes out when her partner wants to know why collection agencies are calling.

When entering a relationship—whether matrimonial, common-law, or same-sex—it is wise to lay some groundwork on financial matters. First and foremost, set up short-term and long-term plans. Do you both want to retire at age 55? How do you get there? Or how do you retire comfortably if one decides to stay at home and raise the kids? For many couples, a joint household account for routine expenses can work well. There can be separate accounts earmarked for a certain percentage of each paycheque that can be used for investing. But before this works, you've got to sit down and discuss it.

Setting up a household budget is also key. And having accurate facts and figures on paper can relieve anxieties and prevent arguments. Try to avoid blaming the other for financial shortfalls—and steer away from bringing up how your parents handled money. The best plan is one without surprises. Keep each other up to date on assets and debts, and what's in savings, chequing, and credit accounts. If disaster strikes, and one or the other is laid off, it is a must to sit down and rework the financial master plan together. Too often, one person takes total control of the bill paying and money management, leaving the other in the dark. This can create doubt and suspicions as to where the money is being spent, and lead to heated arguments. Even your sex life can be affected. Share the responsibilities.

To Stay At Home or Not

Linda is a higher-powered banker, with two children. At one time, both she and her husband headed out to work at the dreaded hour of 6 a.m., fighting rush-hour traffic to get to work, then fighting it to get home again to pick up the kids from daycare.

One day she and her husband decided there must be an easier way. Though the taxman still isn't fair to single-earner families, they decided it would be better if one of them stayed at home. Since Linda was the one who earned the most, they agreed she would go to work, and hubby would stay home. Since then, they haven't looked back.

It's true they can no longer deduct child care expenses, but Linda has peace of mind that her children are with someone they love and trust. But there are other benefits. If Linda was to hire a live-in nanny who also shared in house-keeping duties, she'd be paying her $30,000 a year or more. Not only does she save money, though. Now she saves on time when it comes to grocery shopping and being a taxi service for hockey games, ballet lessons, and trips to the mall. And when the children are sick or need help with homework, it isn't as tough as it used to be when both parents were working. And a bonus: there are hot, home-cooked meals on the table.

Some say this type of arrangement is role reversal, but more and more couples are opting for this option. Of course, sometimes it's the mother who decides to stay at home. The bottom line is that each couple has to sit down and decide what's best for the family, what the budget can accommodate, and who's more comfortable with which role. Maybe both want to work. But remember, children are the treasures of this world. They must be cared for.

To help you decide, here's a survey by Runzheimer Canada which shows how daycare costs across the country can vary. Toronto leads the country with a couple paying $649 per month for a three-year-old child to be placed in a private, for-profit daycare, five days a week, eight hours a day. Ottawa is the second most expensive city at $597 a month, followed by London at $586. Costs were also over $500 in Yellowknife, Montreal and Whitehorse. The least expensive cities were Regina at $343, St. John's at $363, and Saint John at $383.

If one parent does decide to stay at home, remember this: Life insurance through the previous employer may no longer be valid. An at-home parent is a valuable person and expensive to replace. Make sure he or she is covered by insurance.

Yearly costs to replace stay-at-home parents:
- Daycare (child under age 5) $7,500
- Daycare (school-aged child) $3,000
- Housekeeper (once a week) $5,200
- Babysitter (if you work shifts) $9,200
- Take-out meals (once a week) $1,500

TEACH YOUR CHILDREN WELL

Another golden rule of good financial planning is: don't let your children grow up believing there is a money tree for every whim or want. While our schools still let us down when it comes to teaching money management skills, our homes don't have to. Try to involve the children in all planning, even if the subject is financial disaster or divorce. It's a myth to think that hiding problems from them will protect them. Not telling the truth will create fear and insecurity.

Take Lois. After four miserable years of mental abuse from her husband, she finally left with her two sons. Yes, her husband pays supports, but with her annual income of $18,000 a year, money is tight. She wanted her children to grow up knowing the value of a buck, so she's following these guidelines from the Credit Counselling Service of Metro Toronto. Try them with your children, too.

At Age 3:

- Explain what money is and what it looks like.
- Play games to learn to buy and sell things.
- Keep money in a safe place.

At Age 4:

- Identify coins by putting pennies, nickels, dimes, quarters, loonies, toonies, and bills in order.
- When you're shopping, teach them that "when we spend money, it's gone."

At Age 5:

- Teach them how many cents each coin is worth.
- Match small amounts of money with what it can buy.
- Teach them to make choices. "We can't buy everything."
- Teach them where money comes from.

At Age 6:

- Start giving them an allowance they can manage, and set out chores to earn the money.

At Age 7:

- Divide allowance between spending and saving.
- Read price tags with your children.
- Look for items on sale with your children.

At Age 8:

- Teach them how to make simple change.
- Identify times your children blow money on things that don't last.
- Discuss how TV commercials are not real life.
- Start saving trends.
- Teach them how they can earn more by doing extra jobs.

At Age 9:

- Have them tally the cost of several purchases.
- Have them make a simple spending plan for a week, and keep a money diary.
- Help them open a savings account, so they can start to deposit money regularly.
- Teach them about how to co-operate with family efforts to save money on water, gas, food, etc.

At Age 10:

- They should save a small amount each week for a large purchase.
- Help them understand what a cheque is and that it takes money out of the bank.

At Age 11:

- They should be able to calculate the cost of an item including sales taxes.
- Let them borrow money from Mom or Dad for an important purchase, and repay it.
- Make them aware of how peer pressure affects buying decisions.
- They should be saving money for longer periods in a savings account.

At Age 12:

- Teach them how to set up a two-week budget.
- They should be able to classify fixed expenses, versus flexible spending, like a trip to McDonald's.

At Age 13:

- Teach them the beauty of compound interest and how a savings account can grow.
- Teach them the basics of wise investing.
- Buy a blue-chip stock, and teach them how to track its value.
- Warn them about advertising gimmicks, or sales scams, like giving out credit card numbers over the phone.
- Teach them how to shop around, and be comfortable with enquiries over the phone.

At Age 14:

- Have them prepare a personal budget.
- Involve them in saving for education.
- Teach them the costs of running a home—food, telephone, laundry, clothing, car, car insurance, gas, etc.—and involve them in ways to save money.
- Teach them the correct terms of banking transactions.
- Help them set up their own small business enterprise (e.g., grass cutting service, window washing, etc.).

For Lois, whose sons are now 9 and 11, the guidelines are paying off. The children don't expect Mom to hand out money whenever they want it, and they have their regular chores to make money, some of which they're investing. But Lois reminds other women that the best lesson of all for the kids is love. "Being there and letting them know that at all times we loved them, helped us all get through."

WHO'S GOING TO PAY FOR THE KIDS TO GO TO UNIVERSITY?
I often marvel at how some of my sisters have managed to put their kids through university. Take my little sister, Karen. Divorced and having to start all over, not only has she managed to ensure her eldest girl is getting a university education, but she herself went off to York University right in the thick of a separation. Today, displayed proudly on a wall of the new home she just bought with her new partner, Dave, is her Bachelor of Arts diploma. Dad was right. The Leatherdales are good stock. We never say die.

Then there's my older sister, Judi. She and her husband are also putting their eldest daughter through university. The truth is that education these days doesn't come cheap, and for the ones who really want their kids to appreciate it, they'll make the children share in the responsibility of funding.

The Canadian Federation of Students estimates it costs $8,890 a year for tuition, books, rent, and food. If inflation runs at 3%, that means by year 2014, we can expect to be paying $65,000 for a four-year undergraduate degree. And let's not forget about the effect of government cutbacks. Soon, only the wealthy, those on scholarships, or parents who had the wisdom to plan ahead will be able to afford post-secondary education for their children.

How can we afford it? Today, there are two savings vehicles available.

First, there are Registered Education Savings Plans (RESPs), but before the federal government sweetened the RESP pot in recent budgets, most experts advised these babies weren't worth it.

Sure, an RESP allowed money set aside for a child's education to grow tax-free, but before Ottawa changed the rules, if your child decided not to go to university, you only got back your principal investment, not the tax savings.

But now, if your child decides university isn't for her, not only will you get your original investment back, but gains made may be also transferred into your RRSP. But still a problem with RESPs was that, unlike RRSPs, there were no immediate tax deductions. So Judi and Karen were better off investing in their own RRSPs than socking money into an RESP. The only downside was if they withdrew money from their RRSPs to pay for education, they'd pay tax at their marginal personal income tax rate.

Here's how Ottawa has made RESPs even better.

Federal Finance Minister Paul Martin is now offering 20% top-ups to RESP contributions up to $2,000 a year. So, if Judi and Karen were to invest the maximum of $4,000 a year to the new lifetime maximum limit of $42,000, it would add up to $7,200 in gifts from Ottawa. They should crunch the numbers, and see if RESPs are worth it now.

Another popular way to save for the kid's education is to set up an in-trust account in the child's name, but managed by you. If you invest the money in interest-bearing investments, like GICs, the gains made will be added to your income and taxed at your marginal income tax rate.

But if through the in-trust account, you can invest money in investments subject to capital gains, like equities, the gains are attributable to your child, not you. Chances are there will be little, if any, tax to pay.

CHAPTER SIX

Family Finances II: Debt, Scams, and Rip-Off Artists—A Girl's Arch Enemies

WATCH OUT FOR LOAN SHARKS

For Leanne, a 27-year-old single mother, the financial nightmare hit on her daughter's sixth birthday. "My daughter's birthday was one sad day," Leanne recalls. "I couldn't afford food, let alone a birthday cake. "Staring personal bankruptcy in the face, with no money to pay the rent, Leanne didn't know where to turn. Desperate and panicking that she and her child could soon be out on the street, she answered a newspaper advertisement that promised easy money for the financially destitute. Even bankrupts, the ad promised, would not be turned down.

Leanne didn't know it, but she was about to become a victim of scuzzy loan brokers, who've hosed millions and millions of desperate, cash-strapped consumers throughout North America. The loan broker epidemic is so bad that U.S. authorities, including the FBI, have demanded that Canadian authorities clamp down on loan boiler rooms operating out of Canada. Most of them are located in Toronto, but their network is big. These sharks are feasting on the financially down-and-out in almost every part of the continent.

Leanne, who lives in Woodstock, Ontario, swallowed their bait—hook, line, and sinker. All she needed to do was to give them $485 and she'd get a debt consolidation loan for $8,000. Then she'd be back on her feet, and her financial worries would be over. Persistent, these brokers told her she'd been approved for the loan. So she borrowed the $485 from her parents, handed over the money, and waited for her loan to be deposited in her bank account, as promised.

But like all other victims, she never got the money—just obscene language when she kept calling the broker to ask what went wrong. "After they told me I was approved, I couldn't get hold of them," she recalled. "And when I finally did, they told me I was turned down and my fee was non-refundable." Fired up and angry, Leanne fought back. She protested in front of the loan broker's office, she drove to Toronto to tell her story on TV, and she contacted police, government, and me.

Authorities told her I had waged a long, bitter battle with these brokers in column after column in the *Toronto Sun*. After three years of fighting, including protests, and with help from Ontario Liberal finance critic Gerry Phillips, the Loan Brokers Act was passed into law in December 1994. It's known as the "Linda Leatherdale bill" at Queen's Park in Toronto, home of the Ontario Legislature.

Other provinces are planning similar legislation—legislation that makes it illegal to charge upfront fees, no matter how they're disguised, to obtain a personal loan. Not only are these brokers feasting on consumers, but they're now going after small businesses, especially the self-employed who are desperate for start-up cash. So far, several brokers have been fined under the act, but the first to be sentenced to a jail term for ripping off consumers is loan broker kingpin Glasford Alexander, principal of AAA Financial Consulting and First Rate Financial Consulting Inc. Alexander and his wife were found guilty of hundreds of offences under the act, and as I write this, they face even more charges. Alexander's lawyer has appealed the sentence and pleads his client is innocent.

Leanne is now trying to get back on her feet and is doing everything in her power to make life for her daughter better. About her only other chance of recouping her $485 is through small claims court. The important thing to remember is that if you hit rock bottom never, never, never hand over your last penny on the promise of a loan.

CREDIT: The good, the bad, and the ugly

TROUBLE IN CARD PARADISE

Leanne isn't alone in her financial troubles. Hundreds of households carrying record debt loads are barely hanging on. Corporate downsizing, high unemployment, and falling incomes only make it worse.

But there's this reality, too. Too many of us don't understand the real cost of borrowing or the real cost of credit. And many still naively believe an array of credit cards — especially gold-plated ones glistening in our wallets — is a status symbol, when is it probably means the signs of a loser.

Why do I say that? Because some never get it, until it's too late.

Like when they wake up and find they're borrowing against one credit card to make the minimum payment on another. Then they're 30 days, 60 days, and now 90 days late with payments. Then the whole house of cards collapses, and they stare personal bankruptcy in the face.

This is no laughing matter, though there are some individuals who cleverly play the bankruptcy game and never seem to lose out. But the reality is once you've declared bankruptcy, it's usually a rough road for at least seven years when creditors refuse to grant credit, your credit rating hits rock bottom and is difficult to recover, and the stigma of being a financial loser can affect getting or even losing a job. The numbers are staggering. While personal bankruptcies remain at record highs, with 80,000 Canadians throwing in the towel in 1996 alone, there are 50.1 million credit cards in circulation. On Visa and MasterCard alone, we Canadians owe a whopping $20.5 billion.

Add up all debt—like mortgages, bank loans, and auto leases—and never before in our history, have we carried so much household debt while saving so little.

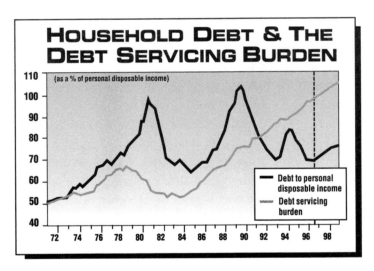

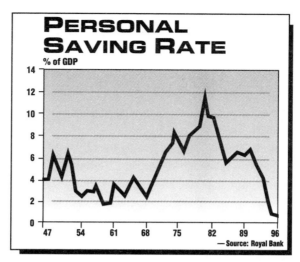

PERSONAL SAVING RATE

% of GDP

— Source: Royal Bank

Living high off the hog of credit during the boom-time, designer-label days of the late 1980s, Canadians carried huge debt loads into a period when the economy collapsed into the biggest economic contraction since the Great Depression. As we lost jobs and suffered falling incomes, our debt loads grew. And so now, after we told governments to get their fiscal houses in order and get rid of debt, total household debt is now more than $500 billion—close to the amount our federal government owes in total debt, despite finally balancing the books in its 1998 budget.

The pattern is clear: Once that monster debt takes on a life of its own, thanks to compound interest, there's no taming it.

When credit card debt, mortgages, bank loans and car leases are added together, total household debt equals more than 100% of disposable income.

That's brutal stuff.

What's interesting is the trend for more and more fiscally minded women to get into the deadly game of credit, and experts say it's because more women are working. In 1977, only 25% of the consumers declaring bankruptcy were women. Today, women make up about 41% of people going bankrupt.

Here are some signs that you could be in trouble:

- **Spending limits on credit cards are at the maximum or are being exceeded.**
- **Credit cards are not being used for convenience, but rather are being used as a necessity.**
- **Cash advances are being taken on credit cards.**
- **Credit is temporarily suspended or permanently revoked.**
- **Money is being borrowed to make it to the next payday.**

- Payments that are being made are the minimum monthly balances or are only for interest and service charges.
- Calls are being received by collection agents, who may threaten to repossess assets or to undertake legal action like garnishment of wages.
- Utilities have been, or are threatened to be, suspended.

CAUGHT IN A CREDIT TRAP

Mary never thought this could happen to her. In fact, for years this teacher-turned-entrepreneur, who believes you pay what you owe, rarely carried a credit card balance. But that all changed in 1998. By spring, Mary was angry, frustrated, and on the brink of tears as collectors kept hounding her and threatening legal action over the $4,000-plus that was outstanding on her Visa card. "I'm paying them when I can," she sighed to me one day. "And I want to pay them, but right now it's really tough. I feel like a victim."

Here's Mary story: Early in life, she wanted to be a teacher, so not only did she go to university in Canada, but she also travelled to the United States and England. In London, she got a Montessori diploma. When she couldn't find a teaching job, she worked in a number of corporations, but by the early 1990s, when corporate downsizing hit the landscape, she found herself laid off. Again, she went seeking a teaching job, but became frustrated. Teachers weren't in hot demand. So, in 1997, she decided to take her $60,000 in life savings and start her own bookstore. To help make her dream come true, she shopped around at all the banks for start-up capital, but like so many other women, she was rejected. Despite a well-thought-out business plan projecting decent profits, the best she could get was an $18,000 renovation loan to get her new store in an upscale area of Toronto, Ontario, ready to open for business.

Her problems began when she dusted off her Visa card and used it to buy books from one of her publishers. "I met with him and I'd forgotten my cheque book," she recalls, "so I put $4,000 on Visa." Mary was carrying no balance on the card, and was trying to pay all bills by cheque. But as every self-employed person can attest, starting out is tough. Cash flow was slim, and she began missing payments. When she did make a payment, often it was less than the minimum amount. The phone calls began, and she claims her pleas for a workable repayment schedule, which included a visit to her bank's customer centre, fell on deaf ears.

Then, almost a year later, the most frightening call of all came, demanding she send back the cut-up credit card and warning that her file was being handed over to a collection agency. "This is the worst it can get," says Duke Stregger, executive director of the Credit Counselling Service of Metro Toronto. By this time, black marks start showing up on credit ratings. The best rating is a R-1. The worst, a R-9.

Mary went to credit counselling service and sought help, which included working out an agreeable way to pay back the credit card debt. She's now clearing off all bills, plus the bank loan, and aims at getting her company debt-free. "I will be successful. I have such a wonderful business and loyal customers." Mary's ending is a happy one, but it was one tough lesson to learn.

YOU CAN RUN, BUT YOU CAN'T HIDE

If, like Mary, you find you're in trouble, the first thing to do is take control. "Stop buying on credit," advises bankruptcy trustee Marvin Zweig. "Then consult your creditors, and let them know your situation immediately." Most creditors, he adds, will allow you to revise the terms of payments. For example, interest may be waived, and a repayment plan struck. Credit counsellors, like the non-profit Credit Counselling Service of Metro Toronto, which is expanding across the country, can help with this.

The key to the whole exercise is sitting down and working on a budget that sets out monthly income and expenses, as well as a complete list of debts and assets. Another must is to try to consolidate debt into a cheaper personal consumer loan or a line of credit. But a word of caution about lines of credit. If you don't force yourself to pay them off, these suckers can go on forever, defeating the savings of a cheaper rate of interest.

What many people don't understand is that when they rack up debt on retail cards, like Canadian Tire, they're paying an obscene rate of interest of 28.8% on outstanding balances. Even when the Bank of Canada rate plunged to a 30-year low of 3.25%, retail cards were still charging 28.8%. As I write this book, the bank rate is back up to 4.5%—which is a whopping 24.3% spread. Even gas cards charge a massive 24%, and some even now charge a late payment fee. As for MasterCard and Visa, some rates are still as high as 18.4%, a 13.9% spread.

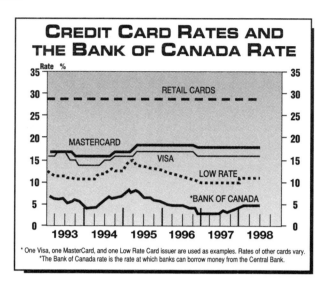

CREDIT CARD RATES AND THE BANK OF CANADA RATE

* One Visa, one MasterCard, and one Low Rate Card issuer are used as examples. Rates of other cards vary.
*The Bank of Canada rate is the rate at which banks can borrow money from the Central Bank.

This book's publisher, former federal Revenue Minister and financial guru Garth Turner, led a probe into the high cost of credit cards in Ottawa. And I, then Business Editor of the *Ottawa Sun*, was at his side, pushing for fairness. But despite this probe, as well as others on Parliament Hill, banks, retailers, and other credit issuers are still free to charge any interest rate they like on outstanding balances, as legislated caps are still frowned upon as a silly, socialist idea that flies in the face of a free marketplace. The only rules governing interest rates are found in the Interest Rate Act, which stipulates that rates higher than 60% are usury.

ARE LOW-RATE CARDS FOR YOU?
One way banks have reacted to a groundswell of complaints—which led to a group of angry Liberals in Ottawa demanding a new government probe—was to introduce new low-rate option cards, carrying interest as cheap as 9%. Sure, these cards are good for women who carry monthly balances. But they may not always save you money. Let me explain:

Did you know that if you're carrying a balance of $300 on a low-rate option card, which charges 9.4% interest plus an annual fee of $24, you're paying $52.20 a year to carry that balance? But let's say you have the same $300 balance on a standard card that charges 15.4% interest, but no annual fee. The cost drops to $46.20. But for women who like to carry large balances, low-rate cards are the way to go. For example, a women who's carrying a balance of $1,500 and switches from a basic card that charges 17.5% to a low-rate card at 9.25% with a $12 annual fee will save $112 a year.

The cost of credit cards

The following is the annual cost of carrying a balance of $300

Low-rate card, 9.4% interest, $25 annual fee.........$52.20

Basic card, 15.4% interest, no annual fee.............$46.20

Basic card, 13.95% interest, no annual fee............$41.85

REWARD OR RISK? YOU DECIDE

Another warning: Don't get caught up in the hype of rewards points cards, which encourage you to spend money just to get a deal on anything from buying a new vehicle, to airplane trips, to retail gift certificates.

"No one who carries a monthly balance should be tempted to use their cards more in order to accumulate reward points," warns Industry Canada's Office of Consumer Affairs.

HEY, GET OFF MY CLOUD

Mary was furious when snarky collection agencies began to bug her day and night. What Mary should know is these persistent folk have rules they have to abide by, and that she has rights, too.

In many provinces, they can call you only between 7 a.m. and 9 p.m. They cannot call on a Sunday or statutory holiday. They cannot make phone calls or send telegrams that you have to pay for. They cannot call so often or say things when they call that it amounts to harassing you or your family. Collection agencies are also not allowed to:

- make you pay more money than you owe
- charge you for their services
- take you to court without warning you ahead of time

They also have to identify themselves, and try to give you a letter that explains they've been hired by your creditor to try to collect money you owe.

If they break any of these rules, fines can be as much as $25,000.

BANKRUPTCY: THE FINAL FRONTIER

A last resort to financial problems is bankruptcy. It's a nasty 10-letter word that can change your financial life. My friend Judy knows this well. Divorced, supporting three boys, and out of work for some time, her bills finally outweighed her ability to pay. Even a credit counsellor recommended Judy throw in the towel.

What bankruptcy does is offer a legal way for immediate relief and protection from creditors who may be threatening to garnishee wages, seize assets, or sue.

The process is also supposed to rehabilitate the debtor, while allowing her to start a new life.

You can declare bankruptcy, if:

- You owe at least $1,000.
- You are unable to meet regular payments when they are due.
- The property you own is insufficient to enable payments of all the debts.

Normally, a person declaring bankruptcy is able to keep furniture, clothing, and personal effects. For Judy, it was a way to start over. Now married again, not only is she debt-free, but she and her hubby have a sizable retirement nest egg.

Twenty-six-year-old Sher, an online producer for a Canadian Internet firm, was also able to start over again, but she didn't have to declare bankruptcy.

It was only two years after she graduated from a Toronto college when Sher found herself in hot water. "I just started to work, and I owed more than $6,000 on my credit cards," she sighed. "I just couldn't manage." Desperate, she didn't know where to turn. But then, one day, while travelling to work on the subway, she saw an advertisement for credit counselling.

She called, and her whole life changed.

"I owed for a student loan, too, and I didn't want to walk away," she recalled. Her credit counsellor helped her set up a budget and repayment plan she could handle. Two years later, she's now debt-free. "It feels so good," Sher chirps in her thirty-third-floor office, overlooking skyscrapers in Toronto's downtown core. "I even have $10,000 in RRSPs."

Her string of bad financial luck has affected her credit rating, but thanks to a friend co-signing for a credit card, she's rebuilding her credit worthiness.

"I feel I have a whole new lease on life," she says with a smile.

WHO'S GOING BANKRUPT?
Believe it or not, there are patterns in bankrutpcy.

According to researchers, people who have limited education and cannot read the fine print, or understand financial matters, may be more apt to go bankrupt. So, too, are young couples who marry early and use credit cards to buy furniture, cars, etc., then with no money set aside for servicing debt, they use more credit to juggle monthly bills. Students, who use student loans to finance their education then can't find a job, also could end up in bankruptcy.

Of course, loss of a job can cause bankruptcy, just as a severe illness can. Financial hardships can also be caused by drug or alcohol abuse, gambling, and compulsive spending.

PROFILE OF A BANKRUPT

- Average age of 41
- Average income of $1,525 a month
- 50% are married with one dependant
- 18% own a home
- 12% declared bankruptcy before
- 4% have a positive net worth
- 35% are unemployed, 15% are self-employed, and 10% are professionals.

Bankruptcy trustee Marvin Zweig explains that the rules are being tightened. For example, it's no longer as easy for students—who account for 25% of all bankrupts, up from only 1% in 1977—to walk away from student loans. As well, in 1998, creditors will be able to oppose the discharging of debts on the grounds an individual has surplus income or could have come up with a viable pay-back proposal. But remember, if you declare personal bankruptcy, it will remain on your credit rating for seven years, making it very difficult or impossible to secure new credit.

I'M NOT GETTING THE CREDIT I DESERVE

Not only do I hear this complaint from legitimate small business operators and the self-employed, but from consumers, too.

Judy was appalled when every bank turned her down for a credit card, even though it was years since she had declared personal bankruptcy. She even pledged to put money into a bank account to cover her credit card limit—they wouldn't budge.

Banks can deny credit for a range of reasons. The biggest, of course, is bankruptcy, which remains a black mark on your credit history for seven years. But even a missed payment or a mistake on your credit rating can cause problems when it comes to trying to secure a credit card or a personal loan.

Over and over, I remind consumers to check their credit ratings. This procedure is free. Just call Equifax at 1-800-465-7166 or Trans Union at 1-800-663-9980. If you find the information on you is inaccurate or incomplete, the agency must either prove its information is correct or delete it from your file. But it's up to you to prove it's inaccurate.

If there are mistakes, it's up to the credit reporting agency to make sure anyone seeing a report within the past six months gets the proper information.

In the United States, the Federal Trade Commission found that 33% of all credit rating reports in that country contained serious errors.

AN INVASION OF PRIVACY?
Many women get upset that their credit and personal history is on record. Most experts will tell us to cool our heels, because there are rules to protect us.

First, no information on you or your credit history is supposed to be available to the public. And if anyone is found guilty of releasing this information, they can pay hefty fines or be jailed.

There are two kinds of reporting agencies. One is a credit reporting agency, which keeps track of your credit transactions and history, like bankruptcies, writs, and judgements. Credit bureaus keep this information on file so landlords and credit issuers can decide your ability to pay rent, borrow money, or use a credit card.

The other type is personal information reporting agencies that collect information on your lifestyle, plus credit transactions. They'll know your character, reputation, health, physical or personal characteristics, as well as if you live in a house, apartment, or on the streets.

Here's what these agencies can't do:

- Keep reports on bankruptcies discharged more than seven years ago. They can't keep information on writs that represent intentions to sue, issued more than a year before the date of the report, unless they're still being actively pursued. Writs more than seven years old cannot be reported.
- They can keep reports on payment of taxes or fines after seven years.
- They cannot keep information on convictions for crimes after seven years, or information about criminal charges that were dropped.

Linda's Tips
Protect Your Rating
Here's how you can protect your credit rating.

- Always pay your bills promptly. If you have a reason for being late with your payment, let the company know.
- Try to pay off any debt quickly. Avoid prolonged "easy terms" and avoid having to refinance at higher interest rates.
- Never sign a blank form. Remember a contract is a legal document. Always read and understand the fine print.

CREDIT DOCTORS JUST QUACKS

Girls, beware. There are some new kids on the scam artist block, and they call themselves credit repairers. What they do is promise to fix your credit rating for a fee, and some will even coach you to lie and make false claims to try to repair bad ratings. In the United States, new laws are now in force that rule upfront fees charged by credit repairers are illegal. As well, credit reporting agencies must have toll-free lines for consumer complaints, and settle any disputes about credit reports within 30 days. C'mon Canada. Let's get tough, too.

Meanwhile, there are things you can do to try to get your rating back in good standing.

Linda's Tips

Get Your Credit Rating Back

Here's how you can repair your credit rating.

- Open up a bank account and deposit $500 to pledge as security for a credit card from the same bank with a spending limit of $500. Then, use this card to re-establish that you're responsible with credit.
- If the banks refuse to touch you, try a trust company or a credit union.
- If you've been turned down everywhere, use high-risk lenders like Avco, Household, or Beneficial Finance. Yes, the rates of interest will be higher, but it's a chance to re-establish credit. Once you've proved your credit worthiness, move to a cheaper establishment.

But, whatever you do, don't say you're no longer a risk, then blow it by maxing out the cards again.

HOW TO GET THE MOST OUT OF YOUR BANK

There's rarely a woman who doesn't shake her head when it comes to record bank profits. "I have nothing against making a profit, but when small businesses and consumers are being killed by service fees and high lending costs, how can they justify this, and in a monopolistic environment on top of it?" snapped a friend of mine. This lady, who owns her own business, feels frustrated by banks' treatment, both as an entrepreneur and a consumer.

Bank profits are staggering. In 1997, the Big Six chartered banks earned a new record profit of $7.48 billion—19% higher than 1996, and they're well on their way to even higher profits in 1998. Meanwhile, Royal Bank wants to marry Bank of Montreal, and CIBC plans to wed Toronto Dominion—proposals that have seen lofty bank share values climb even higher, as speculation grows that politicians in Ottawa, though talking tough, in the end will give these mergers their blessing.

Even I, the unrelenting bank watchdog, bought into the banks and I haven't looked back. My CIBC shares and investment in a fund that invests in five of the banks have enjoyed unbelievable growth. The bottom line is that bank shares now truly are growth stocks, not just conservative, dividend-rich investments.

"People should quit complaining, and get in on the action," advises Canada's stock market guru Fred Ketchen, senior vice-president and director of equity trading at Canadian brokerage house ScotiaMcLeod. Fred points out that bank shares usually double in value every seven years, and those regular bank dividends can be rich and offer a regular income stream.

That's fine for investors, like me, but what about consumers who want to get a better deal when banking? Being told to "shop around" can cause any woman to cast a cynical eye on the advice. When a sector enjoys an oligopoly, are true competitive forces really at work in favour of the consumer?

There is, however, a way to get a better deal and it's called "relationship banking," though be careful not to become a victim of tied selling, in which you're forced to buy a bank product you may not want just to get a line of credit or a loan. In relationship banking, you park all your business under one roof (RRSPs, mortgage, credit cards, deposit accounts, insurance, etc.). Then you're in a position to demand some fair play, like cutting or waiving fees. Like shaving up to 0.50% to even 1% off going mortgage rates. Like cutting insurance premiums. Like getting an unsecured loan at prime plus. Also, if you're lucky enough to be able to maintain a certain level of money in an account, fees will be waived. But when it comes to money on deposit in a bank or investing in RRSPs, I'd say you're better off not leaving a big chunk of money in a savings account with little or no interest just to save on fees.

Don't forget, each bank offers different packages, each aimed at customers' needs. Check them out. There may be one for you that'll save money. Visit their Web sites, and get the details, or drop into a branch.

Linda's Tips for Beating Bank Fees

- If you're a senior or have children, enrol in special accounts that reduce or waive fees.
- Choose a monthly "flat fee" service package that best suits your needs. Some packages can save up to $25 a month and transaction fees can be low as 20¢.
- Consolidate the number of banking accounts with monthly mainte-nance fees to cut costs.
- Open a savings account, separate from a transaction account, and avoid frequent withdrawals from it.
- Accelerate mortgage payments, double up payments, and make pre-payments of up to 10% a year to increase payments by 10% to save on interest costs.
- Ask your bank to waive mortgage renewal fees.
- Sign up for no-fee credit cards.
- Look up banking and personal finance information on the Internet for the best deals.
- Have your pay directly deposited into your account, and maybe get a free withdrawal.
- Check out new telephone banking services that can reduce fees.
- Make purchases with a debit card, rather than cheques that cost 30¢ or more.
- Bundle your bills into one envelope when paying by an automatic banking machine (ATM).
- Try to use your bank's ATM, and avoid an extra fee.

VISIT A WEB SITE

Industry Canada's Office of Consumer Affairs will help you calculate the best deal on service fees. Its Financial Service Charges Calculator can be accessed through Industry Canada's marketplace information Web site, where it com-pares fees at 11 institutions. Also, visit the Canadian Bankers Association Web Site at www.cba.ca or call 1-800-263-0231 for free information.

FORGOTTEN MONEY: MILLIONS LEFT IN DORMANT BANK ACCOUNTS

Ottawa just won a million-dollar lottery. And it's our money the federal government won. On January 1, 1998, the Bank of Canada confiscated $24 million of unclaimed money left in some 189,000 forgotten bank accounts. That's because the government made changes to the Bank Act that allow our central bank to take possession of unclaimed money up to $500 left in bank accounts that have been dormant for 20 years. The limit used to be $100. Today about $150 million of our money is sitting unclaimed in banks across the country.

"This cash rightfully belongs to thousands of Canadian families," says Edward Palonek, president of Found Money International, a firm that specializes in matching the money with its rightful owners. Palonek, from Oakville, Ontario, opened his company after he found it difficult to get information on bank deposits when his parents passed away. His service is so popular across North America, he's been a guest on the Oprah Winfrey and Maury Povich shows. You can visit Found Money's Web site at www.foundmoney.com or telephone his automated phone system at 905-337-CASH (2274). Palonek charges $10 for a search.

Under the Bank Act, chartered banks are required to hold onto dormant accounts for 10 years. After that, a list of those accounts is published in the government's *Canada Gazette* and, if the banks still don't hear from the rightful owners, the money is transferred to the Bank of Canada. In 1997, $4 million in 6,000 dormant accounts on record with the Bank of Canada was claimed and returned.

GETTING FISCALLY FIT: OH WHAT A FEELING

One of the biggest problems many of us have is there's more week than there is paycheque. It's a nagging problem that plagues a working poor West Coast girl, Cheryl, and her hubby, Steve. I call them poor, but they're not really. Steve's a well-paid technician. Cheryl works as a part-time nurse. A bad habit of overspending their paycheques has left them with a massive household debt hangover that's tough to cure. What Cheryl and Steve need is a good financial work-out, which includes a strict household budget they can stick to.

What's amazing, say many credit counsellors, is how high-income earners tend to overspend, how they can get into financial hot water, and how some of them end up declaring personal bankruptcy—a move Ottawa frowns on. But, everyone—including Steve and Cheryl—can learn to live on less and shave thousands off the household budget. Not only will this help pay down debt, but it will free up money for investments that can make their wealth grow and ensure a healthy retirement.

Here are some tricks to do it:

1. Reduce the cost of carrying debt. Consolidating high-cost debt, like credit card debt, into cheaper lines of credit or personal consumer loans can save hundreds of dollars. The cheapest lines of credit are those that are secured with assets, like a house.
2. Shop around for the best car insurance rate, and don't forget to take advantage of any discounts available, like age and safe driving record.
3. Take public transportation instead of driving, which can save hundreds in gasoline and parking expenses.
4. Get the cheapest mortgage money. Going short-term can shave thousands off the cost of a mortgage, and convertible terms allow you the comfort of locking in without a penalty should rates head higher. But be careful. If some economists are right, by the time this book hits the streets, the short-term rates may be as high as long-term rates, which wipes out the advantage of this strategy. If you're locked into a higher rate of interest, you can renegotiate. But banks will charge a penalty of three months' interest, or the interest rate differential, and they'll charge whichever is greatest. The trick here is to sit down and weigh the interest savings against the penalty. If savings are greater, do it. If the penalty is, don't. Also, you can blend and extend, but be careful. You may not end up saving any money.
5. Cut your home heating costs by using an electric thermostat to regulate the temperature. The savings can be awesome.
6. Use an energy-efficient showerhead that can save on the water bill. Put timers on the pool and hot tub heaters.
7. Shop around for house insurance, and consider pooling both house and auto insurance under one insurance roof, to save costs. If you're buying insurance through a bank, move all your business there and demand the savings.

Other Ways to Put Money in Your Pocket

Are you like Wendy, who buys lunch every day? Try making your own lunch, to save $50 a week. Then sock that money in an RRSP. Or how about this? Instead of buying a favourite magazine as you check out at the grocery store, get a subscription and cut the cost in half.

Up in Smoke

It's an alarming fact of life. More and more young women are getting hooked on that dirty and addictive habit of smoking. On average, a smoker will inhale three packs of cigarettes a week. Let's say each pack costs about $3. That's $9 a week, or $468 a year on cigarettes. Now, let's say you're 20 and instead of smoking you invest that $468 in an RRSP at an average annual growth rate of 10%. By the time you hit age 65, you'll have $398,561.

Play RRSPs, Not Lotteries, and Win

We'd rather gamble with our retirement and buy lottery tickets more than RRSPs. The startling numbers are contained in a recent Decima poll commissioned by Royal Trust, which shows some 40% of Canadians buy RRSPs, while 69% buy lottery tickets in hope of a lofty retirement nest egg. Well, here are the cold hard facts. Your chances of winning the big prize of Lotto 649—one of the richest lotteries—are one in 14 million. Yet, in 1993–94, we socked $1.88 billion into nine different lotteries, and we netted only $941 million in "tax-free" winnings.

Now, let's say instead of spending $10 a week on lottery tickets, you took that money and bought an investment under the RRSP tax shelter. In one year, you'd save $520; over 30 years, with an average compounding return of 10%, that would grow to $85,000. Now let's say you're in a 50% tax bracket. You'd also get a $260 tax savings. And if you invested that money, even outside an RRSP at 10%, you'd get another $17,000. That's $102,000 in the bank, guaranteed.

Shop Till We Drop, and Not Go into Debt

Some girls, like one of my best friends, Lesley, gets easily turned off by what I'm suggesting here. But, being a consumer who doesn't like to pay full price for anything, even designer labels, I've found a few tricks. And believe me, the rewards have been great. Read on.

How would you like to get a Simon Chang suit for $26? Or how about a Mr. Jax jacket for $5.99? I even got an Yves Saint Laurent off-the-shoulder, black body suit, worth $250, for $10. And on one outing I found a strapless, sequined cocktail dress for $5 that rivals my one-of-a-kind designer dress from L.A., which set me back a cool $500.

Where am I shopping? Shhhh! Some neat consignment shops, where sometimes you can even score brand-new pieces for bargain-basement prices. I've even been able to scoop up some great finds by getting up early on a Saturday morning and rummaging through people's garage sales.

"I don't know why I'm doing this," moaned an embarrassed Lesley, as we drove from sale to sale one hot summer's morning in my convertible, after I convinced her to join me on an outing. "I hate other people's junk," she sighed.

That morning, I found some great stuff, like a new silver champagne bucket that was still in its box. Its worth? About $75 at Birks. I paid $5. But Lesley, whose wardrobe and home furnishings are nothing but the best, still wasn't convinced.

It wasn't until we were on a trip to Aruba, where we were visiting an upscale shop full of expensive pottery and figurines from around the world, that I may have changed her mind. Mom was with us, and even she couldn't believe what I blurted out.

"Hey, Lesley, look at this," I chirped, pointing to an unusual glass holder for floating candles. The clerk was quick to tell us the price tag was US$125.

"Lesley," I went on with glee, "I have exactly that same candle holder. And I paid 50¢ at a garage sale." Mom, a consummate Scot , smiled.

The lesson is that there are many ways to shave costs from our household budgets, as Mom knows well. Like keeping coupons in a cookie jar by the door and faithfully taking them with you when you grocery shop. Or putting loose change into a bucket for holidays. Or buying next year's Christmas gifts on Boxing Day. The trick is, whenever you save money, take the savings and invest it in something that'll make it grow.

As for those no-money-down, no-interest deals, they're good if you're a disciplined shopper. For example, let's say you buy a wide-screen TV worth $2,600 and you have six months to pay for it. Isn't it better to have that $2,600 in an investment growing, than to pay for it upfront when the retailer is giving you this unbelievable break of no money down and no interest?

But you've got to make sure you have the money when the days of grace are over. Why? Because if you don't, the debt usually goes into the hands of a financial firm whose rates of interest are much higher than those offered by the banks. If you can't pay cash, try for a cheaper consumer loan or a line of credit to pay it off. And whatever you do, don't buy something you don't need just because there's a no-money-down, no-interest deal.

To Lease or to Own

Did you know when it comes to buying a new car, girls rule? But the nagging question we still keep pondering is do we buy or lease? And what about the nasty depreciation as we drive the baby off the lot?

Ruth, a real estate agent, was perplexed about what to do. "Linda, I watched your TV show where you discussed auto leasing. I'm in the market for a new car, and your show made me think about whether I should lease or buy." My advice to Ruth? Before she signs anything, don't swallow any sales pitches. And crunch the numbers for herself. Sometimes leasing is good and works for the consumer, but sometimes buying can be better, I cautioned.

A recent undercover investigation by the Automobile Protection Association, partly funded the Industry Canada, found that more than half the time consumers were being steered into leases that on average cost them $1,500 more by the time the lease was paid off.

To help Ruth, I went to Robert Lo Presti, president of OrangeSoft, a company that sells The CarCalculator, and here's what we found out. Ruth wanted to buy a mid-sized car in the $24,500 range. When we crunched the numbers on a two-year lease at 6.6%, compared to a two-year bank loan at the same rate, we found that Ruth would pay about $1,300 less by buying. The only problem was her monthly car loan payment would be over $1,000. And that's why auto leasing has become more and more popular, growing to a $19-billion business by

1997, compared to only $3 billion in 1990. No wonder our record-profit banks want a piece of this action.

The absolute best deals—and believe me the idle rich are taking advantage of these—are the 0% financing terms some auto manufacturers have been offering. The problem, though, is 0% financing may not apply to the car of your dreams. So shop around, because with these babies, buying will be cheaper than leasing.

"What boggles my mind is how consumers wouldn't take out a mortgage without knowing how much they're borrowing, or what interest rates they're being charged," says Robert. "Yet with auto leasing, all they look at is the monthly payment. Dealers and leasing companies are laughing all the way to the bank." Robert's CarCalculator (www.carcalculator.com) can help a woman crunch the numbers.

Driving for a Tax Write-off

Don't be fooled by those who brag that leasing offers a better tax break than buying. The tax rules are pretty straightforward. Any self-employed person, or a person on contract who's required to use her car for business, can write off a portion of her auto expenses. These include gas, repairs, maintenance, interest, insurance, as well as lease payments or depreciation if the car is bought.

So let's go back to Ruth and her two-year lease versus her two-year auto loan, at 6.6%. With her lease, payments would be $344 a month and that means she could write off $4,128 in the first year, plus $4,128 in the second, for a total of $8,256.

But let's say she takes out the two-year loan, instead. Her total cost would be $28,175, and in the first year, she'd be able to deduct $4,226 in depreciation, followed by $7,185 in the second for a total of $11,411.

Linda's Safe Driving Tips

- Don't be afraid to check out a year-old car on the lot, perhaps one that's been driven by an executive at the dealership. Depreciation on these can be far less.
- If the dealership is offering a sweetheart deal to buy a car, take it. At anywhere from 0% to 3.9% financing, that's cheap borrowing for an asset that usually depreciates and offers little or no tax benefits. Or try to get the best lease with the smallest down payment, smallest monthly payment, and the best "guaranteed" buy-back price. Then take the money you were going to spend and sock it into an investment that offers much higher returns, and even tax savings.

If you do decide to lease, here are some tips from the Automobile Protection Association:

- Make the lowest possible down payment.
- Look for the lowest total cash outlay (down payment plus monthly payments) and don't worry about the end value because, ideally, you should turn the car in at the end of a lease.
- Choose a lease with the end value guaranteed by the auto maker, not you, the consumer.
- Try to find a lease with low interest rates. Interest rate rebates from the manufacturer and high residual values can save hundreds of dollars compared to regular auto lease rates of 9% or more.
- Shop around for a dealer who doesn't charge an administration fee just to write up the lease.
- If a dealership asks you to make a written offer to purchase before providing all the costs for a lease, walk away. If you can't, make your offer "conditional" by writing "subject to acceptance of all terms by the consumer" above your signature.

Don't Be a Victim

Late one night last year, I got a panic call from my sister-in-law Chrissie. She'd just given out her credit card number over the phone to a telemarketer for a vacation on a cruise ship, leaving from Florida. The hitch? She'd have to pay her own way to get to Florida. "When I checked it out, it would be cheaper for me to book through a travel agent," she sighed. When Chrissie called to ask for her money back, she was given the old line. No refunds. Often, these fly-by-nighters are out of business by the time you hit the beach. Whatever you do, never give your credit card number out over the phone.

Then there's Ruth, who fell for this one, hook, line and sinker. When she went to the mailbox one day, she found a letter gleefully stating she'd won a foreign lottery, and her prize was waiting. All she had to do was fill in an information form and pay a $25 administration fee, and her prize would be on its way. She paid all right. The prize never turned up, and her name was on a common list used by scam artists.

A Pyramid for the Girls: The Latest Scam

My girlfriend, Mel, always loves a good time, but seems to be forever in a financial bind. So it didn't take me by surprise when my cell phone rang, and on the line was Mel, with this offer: "Can you meet me and some of the girls for a drink tonight? They want you to join a new women's investment club."

Excitedly, she added, "All you need to do is invest $5,000, and you'll get $40,000 back."

I gasped. How could this be possible, I wondered, and what was the catch with Mel? I asked her what the name of this club was.

"The Women's Investment Network," she chirped. "It's better known as WIN and only women are allowed. That's because we're girls helping girls." She went on, "I don't have the money, so I'm going to get this friend to spot me the $5,000 and we'll share the $40,000. Or maybe you want to be my partner."

My face flushed. This has to be a spinoff of the pyramid scam known as Women Helping Women, which is sweeping women off their feet across the country. I've also heard it called Circle of Friends, as women urge other women to join, saying that it's our turn to show the men up...that we can be good investors. It sure sounds enticing, but it's a scam.

"Mel, listen to me," I said sternly. "Women have been arrested and charged with participating in this illegal scheme. It's an indictable offence to be doing this, and if found guilty you could go to jail for up to two years."

There was dead silence on the line.

"It can't be a scam," she retorted, "it's perfectly okay...they told me it was, and I know people who got their $40,000."

I explained, as in any pyramid, of course some people make money — especially those who start it or get in near the beginning — but in the end a lot of innocent people get hurt when the pyramid collapses.

Here's how this one works. Each pyramid starts with seven women who must find eight more to complete a 15-person pyramid. The cost to get in is $5,000, and each woman is ranked by the date they join. These ladies are advised not to tell their husbands, because this pyramid is strictly for women — and they're coached to share this wonderful opportunity with friends, relatives, and acquaintances.

When eight recruits are found, the lady at the top takes $40,000 and gets out. Then, the 14 other players split into two new groups of seven and start recruiting all over again.

I adamantly told Mel I wanted nothing to do with it, and advised her to do the same. By the time she hung up, I had her convinced. But too many other women have been led like sheep to slaughter by this scheme.

- Advertisements that guarantee jobs for a fee. "These agencies are ripping off those who can least afford it by hundreds of dollars," warns a Better Business Bureau executive.
- Business solicitations that look like an invoice, that you can easily pay by mistake.
- Car resale swindlers. They promise to sell your car, after you give them power of attorney. By doing that, they can sell your car and give you nothing.
- Credit arrangers who promise to take care of your debt problems, and put you further in debt.
- Businesses that use names very similar to charities to get you to give.
- Fitness deals that leave you financially unfit.
- Phony prize pitches, usually over the phone.
- Model agencies, which promise a blossoming new career after you pay big-time for a photography session.
- Repair scams, like contractors who take the money before the repair, and you never see him again.
- Deposits that disappear.

SCAMS ON THE NET

Everywhere you surf on the Internet, someone has a deal—like make millions through a pyramid deal or buy a cure for cancer.

The Fair Business Practices Branch of Ottawa's Competition Bureau recently surfed the Net and found at least 400 sites with questionable claims. Authorities are clamping down, but consumers should be careful. If it's too good to be true, it's a scam.

How to avoid being scammed:

- Don't ever fall for their lies and assume you've already won something.
- Make sure you read all the details, including the fine print, in any promotional material.
- Don't send upfront money to get a promised prize.
- Don't reveal a bank account or credit card number over the phone.
- If a firm sends a demand letter threatening legal action for non-payment of lottery tickets you never bought—go ahead, make their day—call them and demand proof. Even threaten them with legal action. Keep copies of all the correspondence.
- Be on guard, and don't offer information that could put you on a list for further telemarketing fraud.

- If in doubt over a lottery, contact local gaming or licensing authorities. Many charities, like hospitals or service clubs, run sweepstakes and lottery promotions for fundraising. They must have government authorization, and a proper licence.

LET ME OUT!

Veronica was in a sweat. Lured in by a flyer that came to her home offering free workouts at a local gym, she went in and signed on the dotted line. "I'm 20 pounds overweight, I needed to get into a fitness routine, and this sounded so good," she explained, as we sipped our espressos after a light lunch. "But now that I read the fine print, I feel I'm being taken." What can Veronica do?

Whether it's a health or fitness club, a modelling agency, sports club, dance lessons, even martial arts training, there are ways to get out of a contract. First, is the contract valid? Laws in Ontario rule it isn't if it doesn't list:

- Your name, address and the name and address of the agency
- The services you'll be receiving
- The guarantees, if any, or a statement that there are no guarantees
- The number and amount of payment instalments
- Extra charges for paying by instalment

Contracts for prepaid services can last no longer than a year. Also, most provinces rule a contract is not valid if you were cheated, misled, or taken advantage of by a salesperson. There are also rules about over-charging, imposing unfair terms, and selling services, like a repair service, when they're not needed.

Linda's Tips

Know What You're Signing

- Read the contract from beginning to end, including the fine print.
- If you need time to think about the terms and understand everything the contract says, don't sign. You may want to consult a lawyer.
- If there are points you don't agree with, draw a line through them and initial them. Then get the sales staff to initial, too.
- If you're promised something that's not in the contract, get the salesperson to write it out on company letterhead.
- Never cave in to pressure.

CHAPTER SEVEN

Give Me Shelter: Homes Still a Great Asset

People always ask me: Is real estate still worth it? I find this an intriguing question, because a home for most Canadians is not just an investment. It's a comfort zone. It's a place to raise the kids. It's a place to enjoy retirement. In short, it's a little piece of paradise, where landlords and the taxman don't rule. And as Re/Max so bluntly puts it, you can't sleep in your mutual fund.

Personally, I love real estate. It's like owning a piece of this wonderful country, and unlike paper investments, you can walk it, renovate it, design it, and develop it into a dream come true. It offers pride of ownership and your own piece of paradise.

For the record, my younger brother Don has made his fortune in real estate, and is now an owner/broker of a Re/Max franchise in Orillia, Ontario. I'm so proud of him.

What especially warms my heart is that his partner, Don Whitfield, is an entrepreneur extraordinaire and was one of my dad's best friends. There's nothing I love more than sipping a glass of wine or two and smoking a cigar with Don, as he reminisces about his days with my dad.

Even before my brother ventured into this important sector of the economy, I had a thing for real estate. I could spend endless hours poring over listings or taking jaunts into the country in search of the perfect spot that one day I'd own. Today, even though I own my own home, I still walk into open houses, and I'll force my brother to show me listings even when he knows I'm not buying.

I still lust after a particular lavish, upscale three-storey freehold townhome, with sunrise views over Lake Ontario, marble and oak floors, and a unique floor plan. When first built at the height of a real estate boom in the late 1980s, it sold for well over $700,000. But as real estate crashed into deflation, the group of investors who bought the unit decided they could no longer hold on. By

1995, after it sat for months with a for sale sign out front, it finally sold, for under $400,000. My heart was broken. I missed the deal of the century, a chance to put my money where my mouth is and become a real estate investor, not just a home owner.

In the spring of 1998, a real estate agent called. "Linda, one of those lake-front townhomes finally listed again. Do you want to see it?" My heart skipped a beat. "Yes, yes," I said eagerly. He said he'd set up an appointment. Hours later he called back. "I'm so sorry, it sold." What a change in the market. It listed Friday night and was sold by noon Saturday. And for $30,000 over the asking price of $469,000. Real estate was definitely back.

THE DREAM LIVES ON

Everywhere I go in this country, I meet women who still believe in the dream of home ownership, who want a piece of the action, and who crave that comfort zone.

Like Nicole, a TV producer, who was on the line to me, bubbling with enthusiasm: "Sorry, Linda, I haven't been in touch, but guess what—I just bought a home!" She was ecstatic. Only weeks earlier, as we produced a segment for "City Pulse News," we were in her rented duplex in downtown Toronto. The neighbourhood was charming, the layout perfect for her needs, but the landlord was not selling. In the end, Nicole put in an offer for a similar duplex a few doors away. It was a bit of a beater, but she knew that, with renovations, this would be her dream home. Amazingly, at the same time Nicole was making the biggest purchase of her lifetime, so too was a co-worker, Colleen. As dawn broke over Toronto one cold October morning, casting shadows of golden sunlight over the city's skyscrapers, she blurted it out. We were on the floor of City TV's newsroom, and when we took a commercial break, Colleen cooed, "I bought my first home." She went on, "I've been listening to you, and it just made so much sense to buy a home." A week later, after her deal closed, she brought in photos. It was a charming, quaint home in Toronto's east end.

What Colleen and Nicole realized was that after being shut out of Toronto's expensive market in the late 1980s, this was one of the most affordable times to buy a home. Studies everywhere showed it. Right across Canada, the carrying costs of home ownership had fallen dramatically. Why? Because for the first time in post-war history, home prices had fallen into deflation—a plague that sparked some doomsayers to preach, "Real estate is dead." At the same time, mortgage rates fell to 30-year lows, cutting the carrying costs almost in half.

In high-priced Toronto—once the most expensive city in North America in which to buy a home, when in one steamy month in 1989 average prices skyrocketed to $289,000—the turn-around was drastic. Back then, only 6% of renters could afford to get into the market with the cost of servicing home ownership eating up 70% of median pre-tax income. By 1996, more than 30% of renters could afford to buy, as those costs fell to 40% of median pre-tax income.

The Bank of Montreal's housing attractiveness index underscored the trend. By 1997, the index—which tracks the carrying cost of a starter home compared to renting—hit a 28-year high. No wonder homes were hot again. Right across the country, it was now, on average, 21% cheaper to carry the cost of buying a starter home than to rent a three-bedroom apartment.

For a Toronto renter, the Bank of Montreal's index shows a $96-a-month financial edge for the homeowner. A breakdown shows the monthly interest component cost for a $196,000 starter home at $875 a month, compared to the average rent of a three-bedroom apartment at $971.

In every nook and cranny of the country, a first-time-buyer feeding frenzy was in the works, sending sales to near record levels almost everywhere. Today, the move-up buyers are coming back, and as demand outstrips supply, in some desirable areas, bid-ups are happening again. But it's a balanced and healthy market, not a bubble. If you believe in the golden rule—buy low, sell high—timing is perfect for first-time buyers. On the other side of the fence, though, are those who believed that Toronto's real estate bubble of the late 1980s would never burst. What a painful experience. First, the value of their biggest asset was cut almost a third or more, then a stock market meltdown threatened their RRSP portfolios.

Believe me, as Toronto's average prices crashed to a recession low of $192,406 in February 1996, many a marriage didn't make it. That's because many couples leveraged themselves to the hilt, taking out high-ratio mortgages based on double incomes. Not only did their homes take a hit, but so too did their jobs, as re-engineering hit the corporate landscape and our unemployment rate shot up to double digits. Some could no longer afford servicing home ownership. Then a bigger reality check hit as they went to renew mortgages. Their mortgages were worth more than their homes. The stress of dealing with this hard fact damaged many marriages as dreams were shattered.

Banks didn't want to take over these homes, so they worked with their clients. But those who had high-ratio mortgages (less than 25% down payment), or who took out a builders' mortgage, or went to a private lender for a second mortgage, faced the horror of possibly being turned down at renewal time.

One morning in 1995, a brown envelope landed on my desk at the *Toronto Sun*. When I opened it, out poured a record number of real estate listings that were powers of sale. An agent obviously wanted me to know the truth of the pain and suffering out there. While Vancouver's real estate prices were going through the roof, thanks in part to an influx of Asian immigrants who were fleeing Hong Kong, the rest of Canada was sinking into deflation for the first time in our post-war history.

It stunned many and brought down even the richest of Canadian families, who convinced big banks to back them in high-leveraged real estate deals. This was, after all, the first time since the Great Depression that Toronto real estate was not reporting year over year gains. Even during the recession of the early 1980s, Toronto real estate had held up, unlike Alberta and British Columbia where housing markets collapsed. This time, big players like the Reichmanns, Robert Campeau, and others were not to be spared. Nor were real estate biggies like Bramalea.

This, combined with demographics showing Canada's population is aging, is why some no longer believe in real estate as an investment. After all, if by 2025, 19.5% of Canada's population will be older than 65, who's going to buy your home? And by 2075, that grey-haired crowd will grow to 22.5% of our population, up from 12% in 1995.

Well-known Canadian demographer David Foot, co-author of *Boom, Bust and Echo*, was quoted in a Vancouver newspaper as saying, "If you have a house today, I'd sell it now." But some say Foot is wrong. Like David Baxter of The Urban Futures Institute: "The myths of the vanishing purchaser and the vanishing tenant are wrong. They are wrong because they take something true (a future decline in the number of 25- to 34-year-olds in Canada) and draw false conclusions (a future decline in the demand for ownership and rental housing)," David states in a recent study. Using Statistics Canada population projections, David concluded that "the demand for ownership and rental residential real estate will increase continuously throughout the next century, with most of the growth occurring in the next 50 years."

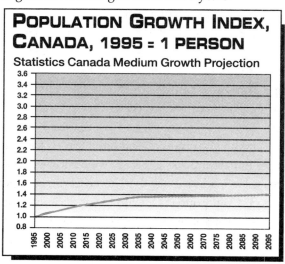

POPULATION GROWTH INDEX, CANADA, 1995 = 1 PERSON

Statistics Canada Medium Growth Projection

Time will tell who's right. But here's my argument: Most of the women reading this book won't be alive by 2075 and will be cashing out equity in their homes long before any crisis—if there is one—hits. Also, many may never want to cash out, although they may buy down (getting a smaller home) or move right out of a major centre where prices are higher to buy in communities that cater to seniors for much cheaper costs.

We must all remember that home prices are simply a reflection of supply and demand—and so many things can factor into the equation. One reason I don't buy Foot's line is because of what happened on Canada's West Coast. Simply put, immigration caused Vancouver's prices to shoot up to the most expensive in Canada while the rest of us wallowed in deflation. Hong Kong investors flocked there, as the land lease expired on their homeland in June 1997, with Communist China taking over. But even when prices in suburbs near downtown Vancouver shot up to more than $350,000, these Asian immigrants regarded them as cheap, cheap, cheap compared to the million-dollar prices they were used to. But now the Asian flu has brought a reality check to Far East real estate. As banks and brokerages failed, the bubble burst and prices crashed.

REAL ESTATE'S TURN TO SHINE

What's ahead for Canada's real estate market?

I find that real estate is very cyclical in nature, and like some believe that U.S. presidential elections affect the stock markets; I also believe there's a relationship between Vancouver's and Toronto's markets. Over the years, I've watched this trend: When Vancouver's in the dumps, Toronto shines, and vice versa. Well, friends, it's happening again in the late 90s. While Vancouver's high prices are dropping, Toronto's are now heading up. But again I stress, this is a healthy recovery, not a speculative bubble.

According to real estate biggie Royal LePage, Vancouver's average house price will drop 2.2% in 1998 to $273,469, while house prices in Toronto's hot market are expected to jump 5.5% from $211,000 to $222,605. By April, we were close with average prices at $222,194.

Canada's leading real estate analyst Frank Clayton still believes that within the next few years, Toronto's prices will be back to their 1989 boom-time peak. That's not a bad return on your money. And don't forget, gains made on selling principal residences remain tax free, although we are not allowed to deduct our mortgage interest, as homeowners in the United States are allowed to do. If you're selling a second residence, like a cottage or an investment property, an increase in the value is subject to capital gains, which means 75% of the gain will be taxed at your marginal personal income tax rate. But if you own an investment property, the mortgage interest is deductible.

Making the Dream Come True

There's no doubt about it. The dream of home ownership lives on in Canada. Nicole knows it, Colleen knows it. So do the 322,973 Canadians who are expected to buy a home this year. So, too, do governments. And they also know how important home ownership and this valuable sector are to our economy.

When people buy homes, they also buy big-ticket items like furniture, appliances, maybe even a car, which all creating valuable jobs. When real estate shines, the economy does well. When it falters, all sectors seem to falter, too. That's why governments have in place programs to help us buy. And the smart woman needs to know how to access them, to help her dream of home ownership come true.

Yes, You Can Put Only 5% Down, But It Will Cost You More

Maggie loves Canada's 5% down scheme, which allowed her and her fiancé to buy their first home with a mere 5% down payment. The couple's dilemma was this. They really wanted to buy their dream English cottage in a small village, outside Toronto, Ontario, before prices headed up, but didn't have the conventional 25% down payment required by the banks. So they decided to go for what the industry calls a high-ratio or "low down payment mortgage"—which requires an insurance premium.

It used to be that the smallest down payment the federal government allowed was 10%, and these were insured through a federal agency, Canada Mortgage and Housing Corp. (CMHC), or the now defunct Mortgage Insurance Company of Canada. But in the early 1990s, Ottawa changed the rules and gave birth to CMHC's new First Home Loan Insurance Program, which allowed a down payment of as little as 5% of the purchase price. Over the years, there have been changes, but the biggest was in spring 1998. That's when CMHC decided the 5% deal would be extended to move-up buyers, not just first-time buyers. But with the change came higher fees.

This is very important to Maggie, because it means big bucks. Why? After May 11, the insurance fee jumped from 2.5% to 3.75%. And it didn't take long for CMHC's new competitor, private insurer GE Capital Mortgage Insurance Canada to match the fee hike. Let's take a closer look:

Maggie bought her English cottage for $180,000, and with 5% down, was carrying a mortgage of $171,000. At the old 2.5% insurance fee, the insurance cost was $4,275. But with the new calculation of 3.75%, this fee jumps to $6,412.50.

Most buyers can't afford to pay the insurance fee upfront, so they roll it into their mortgage. At a 6.5% mortgage rate, the interest payable on the insurance now jumps from $4,317.68 to $6,474.32. And paid monthly, it would cost

Maggie $42.95, not $28.63. Luckily, Maggie and her hubby-to-be got in before the May 11 deadline and are paying the cheaper fee. My advice is to try to get at least a 10% down payment so you have to pay only 2.5%. If you don't have the cash, seek love money from Mom and Dad, the outlaws, or someone you're close to, and draw up a signed promise to repay.

MORE 5% DOWN RULES

The maximum mortgage allowed under the program is $250,000 and applies to cities like Toronto and Vancouver. Elsewhere, the limit ranges from $125,000 to $175,000, depending on where you want to buy. This plan has been widely popular and, perhaps, even a little abused when some zealous builders teamed up with the Home Buyers' Plan to encourage buyers to perhaps take on more debt than they should.

But Ottawa has now tightened up these sweethearts. For 5%-down deals, no more than 32% of gross family income can be used on paying the principal, interest, taxes, and other costs, like heating. The total debt servicing costs for the new homeowners under this plan cannot exceed 40%. Also, any gifts these buyers may receive, let's say from parents, to help them meet the cost of the 5% down payment, must now be in their hands before making an application for mortgage insurance. The buyers must also prove to CMHC that they have the 1.5% of the purchase price to cover closing costs. The buyer must also qualify for a five-year mortgage term, but can take out a term of no less than three years. Any CMHC office will give you details of this plan.

THE RRSP HOME BUYERS' PLAN

I'll never forget how I got burnt by Ottawa. As a very young journalist earning a modest salary, I wanted to save for a home. Back then, the best way to do that was under the federal government's Registered Home Ownership Savings Program, which allowed my investments to grow tax free in order to buy a home. Thinking I was doing the right thing, I religiously socked money into the plan.

Years later, when I was working for the *Edmonton Sun*, the father of the GST, former Finance Minister Michael Wilson, pulled the plug. Up in smoke went this valuable plan. At my bank, I was told the only way to continue to protect my money from the taxman was to move it to my RRSP. This ended up being bad advice, and did I pay the price! When I finally decided to buy, in order to get conventional financing, I was forced to cash in some of my RRSP money. And I paid thousands of dollars in tax at my marginal income tax rate. Angry? You betcha. Well, we no longer have to worry about this. That's because in

February 1992, Ottawa finally woke up to the realization that homes should be part of a retirement plan, and the Home Buyers' Plan was born.

The federal government now allows you to use up to $20,000 of your RRSP nest egg "tax free" (or $40,000 if you're a couple) to buy a home. At first, it was just a one-year plan, which allowed the money to be used for both first-time and move-up buyers. You could either buy a home or build one. But when Ottawa extended the plan in the 1994 budget, the rules were changed so that only first-time buyers could take advantage of the program. To qualify, the buyer could not have owned a home for five years. If you have a spouse and he owned a home that you both occupied during that time, you are disqualified.

In the 1998 federal budget, the rules were changed again so that those who already owned a home, but wanted to buy a home more accessible for a disabled or dependent relative could also use their RRSP money tax free.

Meanwhile, all types of real estate qualify—single-family homes, condos, free-hold townhomes, apartments in duplexes. The only criteria: It must be an owner-occupied, principal residence. What a popular program this has been. Since 1992, some 500,000 Canadian households have taken advantage of it, by withdrawing an average of $9,460 or a total of $5 billion from their RRSPs. That puts the total mortgage debt under the plan at $355 billion.

Now, here's what neat: The money has to be invested in the RRSP for only 90 days before you can take it out. So, if you're planning on buying a home, it may be wise to make as big a contribution as you can to get the tax savings. The only downside? After two years, plus whatever months are left in the current year, you must begin to repay that money into your RRSP in 15 equal annual instalments. If you've taken on too much debt, and find you cannot afford to make the repayment, the taxman will be there to tax the amount at your marginal income tax rate.

Also, remember—when you make the repayment into your RRSP, you won't be allowed the same tax relief, i.e., you won't be allowed a tax deduction again at tax time. But once the money is back in the plan, the investment starts to grow again without the taxman getting his hands on it. Some experts argue against taking money out of an RRSP and losing the benefit of compound interest. But others point out you can actually save money when you use your RRSP money to make a bigger down payment.

Let me explain: Let's say Nicole is taking out a $100,000 mortgage with her bank for 25 years and the average mortgage rate is 8%. That means in any one year she'll make $9,158.52 in mortgage payments. But let's say she takes $20,000 out of her RRSP and reduces the mortgage to $80,000. Now, her annual mortgage payments total $7,326.96 for a savings of $1,831.56.

But let's not forget she has to pay the money back into her RRSP in 15 equal annual instalments. For Nicole, that's $1,333 a year. So her total savings amounts to $500 by using her RRSP money. If Nicole had left that $20,000 in her RRSP, at an average rate of 10%, by the time she was 65, it would have grown to $295,700. Even after she repays the $20,000 into her RRSP, it will only grow to $168,472. Here's how she can win. Let's say she takes the $500 savings she nets each year with the life of her 25-year mortgage and socks it into an RRSP. It would then be worth $296,015 by the time she's 65. And Nicole would be ahead by $315.

All Revenue Canada offices offer details on this popular plan.

GOVERNMENTS WANT YOU TO BUY

Different provinces offer different plans to help home buyers buy their first home. In Ontario, it was the Ontario Home Ownership Savings Program (OHOSP), but be warned—former NDP premier Bob Rae scaled back this baby so much, it's really no longer worth using it. My bet is you're better off with the feds' RRSP Home Buyers' Plan. But what's real cool is Premier Mike Harris's Land Transfer Tax Rebate that can save up to $1,725 in taxes for a first-time buyer of a brand-new home.

Check with your provincial government for your province's plans. For information on the OHOSP, call 1-800-263-7965.

HOME-BUYING TIPS

For women like Maggie, who are taking the plunge for the first time, home buying can be a stressful, albeit, happy experience. Too often, buyers jump in on impulse, and forget to do their homework. The first thing any smart girl should do is get to a bank and get pre-approved. Not only does this tell you how much house you can afford, but it locks in today's mortgage rates for 60 to 90 days. Make a list of things you want, and decide where you want to live. A good real estate agent is important, as is a lawyer you can trust. Always, always have your lawyer check out everything before you sign. If you're buying a new home, check out the reputation of the builder. If it's a resale home, hiring a home inspector is a good idea. When it comes to making an offer, remember a firm offer is just that. Firm, and with no conditions. A conditional offer, however, means certain conditions must be met before the offer's accepted. Make sure you're paying a fair price, by getting information on sales of similar homes in same neighbourhood.

How to Put Money in Your Pocket, Not the Bank's

There's nothing really complicated about this: The faster you pay down your mortgage, the more money you put in your pocket, and the less the bank gets. Here's a simple scenario: Let's say you have a $300,000 mortgage, and you took 25 years to pay it off at an average mortgage rate of 8%. At the end of the 25 years, the mortgage will have cost you $686,892. Why? Because $386,892 is interest you pay the bank. And guess what? If you're in a 50% tax bracket, you'd have to earn $772,000 to pay the interest and the principal because in Canada mortgage interest in non-deductible.

Now let's say you cut the amortization period of the mortgage in half, to 12.5 years. That same $300,000 mortgage at 8% would cost only $472,278, with $172,278 going to the bank in interest payments. That's a 55% savings in interest.

A trick here is to cut your mortgage's amortization, but keep the payments the same. That way you pay even less in interest. And that's smart money management. Remember, today's consumers are truly in the driver's seat when it comes to our hot, competitive mortgage industry, so don't be afraid to shop around, and get the best deal. Banks commonly shave 1/2% off rates to get you in the door. But time and time again, I've written about the persistent, smart consumer who understands relationship banking and isn't afraid to move all her business (RRSPs, lines of credit, etc.) under one roof and get up to 1% off going mortgage rates. (See Chapter 6.)

Be persistent.

A Game of Rate Roulette

One of the hottest questions on the minds of anyone buying a home or renewing a mortgage is "Do I go long term or short term?" This is a tough question to answer, because no one can say for sure where mortgage rates are heading. As I write this, rates are higher, with short-term rates very close to their long-term counterparts. Some even believe the days of 30-year-low mortgage money are over, though nobody is predicting rates to break through the 10% threshold again. But most analysts agree that with little or no inflation, our low mortgage rates will not start to creep up too severely. Nor will we be facing a crisis like the one in 1982, when five-year rates shot up to 22%, and angry homeowners stormed Parliament Hill demanding a moratorium on mortgage renewals.

You can save thousands of dollars in interest payments by playing the short-term game. But do you like playing Rate Roulette, or do you want to lock in and sleep at nights? Canada's mortgage king, Tom Alton of the Bank of Montreal, always offers this advice: If you've just bought a home, and have a little equity in it, lock in for the long term. Then to pay it down more quickly, take advantage of pre-payment options, which allow clients to make one-time lump-sum payments against the mortgage without penalty. Most banks also allow regular payments to be topped up by up to 20% without penalty. That means more money goes towards principal and less interest is paid. Tom's advice to homeowners who have a lot equity and little mortgage left to pay off is play the short-term game. There are many mortgage options to choose from, like convertible mortgages, which offer cheaper rates, but also the convenience of locking in should rates shoot up.

Linda's Tip
A Win-Win Mortgage
If you plan on buying a home, get to a bank right away and get pre-approved. Not only does this help you decide how much house you can afford, but it locks in today's rates for anywhere from 60 to 90 days.
If rates head higher, you're protected. But if they fall, you'll get what's cheapest. It's win-win.

TO RENEGOTIATE OR NOT
When mortgage rates were falling in the early 1990s, renegotiating a mortgage became the hot thing to do. And no wonder. By 1997, mortgage rates were at record lows. But renegotiating can be expensive and wipe out any interest savings. So be careful. What banks will charge you to get out of a mortgage is the interest rate differential (the difference between the rate you've locked in at and the going rate at the time of re-negotiation) or a three-month interest rate penalty. Believe me, the bank will charge whichever is the greatest.

The trick here is to sit down and crunch the numbers for yourself. If the penalty wipes out the savings, don't do it. And remember, the penalty becomes less as you get closer to your renewal. But here's something not to forget: If you have a CMHC-insured mortgage, after the third anniversary of the mortgage, by law the bank can charge only the three-month interest-rate penalty. In the early 1990s as mortgage rates were falling, many banks were not playing fair and were charging the interest rate differential on these mortgages. Know your rights.

As for what's called "blend and extend"—both Alton and Toronto real estate lawyer Alan Silverstein warn it rarely works out in the consumer's favour. "What you're doing here is re-packaging the penalty at the expense of the current rate," warns Alan. "Often, this produces no savings at all."

PAY DOWN A MORTGAGE? INVEST IN RRSPS? OR BOTH?

Another popular question homeowners ask me is this: "Do I pay down my mortgage? Invest my money in RRSPs? Or both?"

Let look at Ruth's situation. She is 20 years away from retiring at age 65 and still owes $150,000 on her mortgage, which at a 7.5% rate will take her 22 years to pay off. Her marginal tax rate is 40% and is expected to be 25% when she retires. She wonders, "Is it better for me to put $4,000 into an RRSP this year, or pay down my mortgage?" Let's take a closer look: If she socked the $4,000 against her mortgage she'd be eliminating 16.68 monthly payments for a total savings of $15,248. But if she invested that same $4,000 into an RRSP, at an average growth rate of 8%, she'd have $18,644 at age 65. At a 40% income tax rate, she'd also get a $1,600 tax savings when she filed her tax return. So, let's say she took the $1,600 tax savings and applied it against her mortgage. That would save her $6,338 in monthly mortgage payments. Now, let's remember her $18,644 in RRSP money is pre-tax income. If she was to cash out at a 40% tax rate, it would be worth $11,186. Now add her $6,338 in mortgage savings with the $11,186, and she's ahead by $17,524 by investing $4,000 in an RRSP and using her $1,600 tax refund to pay down the mortgage. That's better than the $15,248 she would save by using the $4,000 to just pay down the mortgage. This works for Ruth, but your situation might be different. Play with the numbers and see what works for you.

Some institutions, like Canada Trust, offer special deals to help clients pay down mortgages and invest for retirement. Canada Trust was offering 85¢ for every $1,000 in a mortgage to be automatically invested for 12 consecutive months to buy Canada Trust mutual funds. On a $100,000 mortgage, that was $85 per month for a total of $1,020. Not a bad way to save.

HOW TO MAKE YOUR HOME AN INCOME STREAM

Wanda never realized what an asset she had in her family's beautiful stone mansion on the shores of Stoney Lake, near Peterborough, Ontario. The mansion is home to Wanda and her husband, Rompin Ronnie Hawkins, a rock 'n' roll legend, who, though born in Arkansas and an international star, made Canada his home.

I first met Ronnie just before his sixtieth birthday bash at Massey Hall in Toronto, where such legends as The Band, Carl Perkins and Jerry Lee Lewis showed up to party with him.

Over a drink, I convinced Ronnie that if he loved Canada so much, he should be part of my tax crusade. He agreed and performed at Queen's Park where we held our Stop the Tax Madness rally.

Later, he invited me, along with journalists from across North America, to come to Washington, where President Bill Clinton invited him to perform after his "Let It Rock" album, recorded at the sixtieth birthday bash, went gold. Clinton, also from Arkansas, wanted to congratulate his buddy.

So there we were in the Canadian Embassy, with Hawkins and guitarist Jeff Healy, who brought down the house.

It was there I first met Wanda, a stunning lady who once represented Toronto in the Miss Canada pageant. With her youthful exuberance, one would never know she'd been married for so long.

Back in the early 60s, Wanda met her husband-to-be at the Concord Tavern on Bloor Street in Toronto, where he was performing with his band.

"I thought he was a doll," she recalls. "He charmed me with his southern way." Thirty-six years and three children later, the couple are still in love. Two of the children, Robin and Leah, have followed in Ronnie's footsteps. Though rock 'n' roll conjures up images of a retirement of rich royalties and a yacht in the South Pacific, the reality is that at 63, Ronnie's singing the I-Ain't-Got-No-Dough-Re-Mi-Blues. "Rock 'n' rollers don't have retirement plans," explains Ronnie, who's never invested in an RRSP and who has no stocks, bonds, or mutual funds. His biggest asset is the family home, which sits on 200 acres with two and a half miles of shoreline and is estimated to be worth $7 to $8 million. His classic car collection is worth up to $200,000. So as Ronnie enters semi-retirement, they're turning their biggest assets into an income stream. The stone mansion is now a charming bed and breakfast, full of Ronnie's memorabilia. A recent guest is food industry tycoon, Don Tyson, who's a buddy of Ronnie's and whose Tyson Food empire is worth some $6 billion.

"You never know who just might drop by," comments Wanda. "When Ron's not on the road, he misses contact with people, and this is such a beautiful place to share."

Tax accountants will tell you a bed and breakfast is the ultimate "home" business. That's because the entire home, except family bedrooms, can legitimately be allocated as space used for your business, meaning more tax deductibility. And more? If meals are served to guests, food costs and well as home operating expenses can be deducted.

My mom also made her home into an income stream. But, unlike the Hawk and his wife Wanda, she didn't go for a bed and breakfast. Instead, she began renting out an upstairs apartment. Many people are doing this, but the question that needs to be answered is whether this will change how the taxman views your home. In other words, if you rent out part of your house, is it still deemed a principal residence for which you are not required to pay tax on the gains?

Lawyer Alan Silverstein explains, "As long as you don't claim capital cost allowance, which is depreciation, then for tax purposes, it's still considered a principal residence." He adds that your home will be considered an investment property if you rent out more than half of it. Also, make sure the apartment is legal and meets both fire and hydro standards. "If not, and there's a problem, your insurance may not cover any damage."

THE STRATEGY: IS IT FOR YOU?

Some financial gurus argue that strategies of pulling equity out of your home and investing it in higher yielding instruments are the best way to build up assets. In fact, there's even a way to make your mortgage interest deductible, if you remortgage and use the money to buy investments, like stocks, mutual funds, a business, or income-producing real estate. Or you can hold your mortgage in your RRSP. For astute investors, not afraid of risk and the fees involved, this can work. But to those who don't have a high risk tolerance, and especially, seniors, I say be careful.

First of all, it's true that the value of our homes sank in the early 1990s while stock markets soared to new record highs. But if my crystal ball is right, we hit bottom in 1996 and homes are again returning gains. Meanwhile, the cost of remortgaging is heading up again. And the stock markets have suffered a meltdown, with some experts warning that the bears have overtaken the bulls. In other words, those unbelievable stock returns may not be back for a year or so.

It's true that even with a meltdown, equities, over the long term, will yield higher returns on your money. But seniors, who are living off the retirement nest eggs, should now be in more conservative investments. There are three strategies for getting some money out of your house. One is to sell the home and invest the money. The other is to take out a home-equity loan on some of the equity in your home and invest. And the third is tapping into your home equity, with a mortgage from your RRSP. How? As I explained earlier, we're allowed to hold a mortgage on our principal residence, with our RRSP as the lender.

But here's a warning: It will take a couple of thousand dollars to set up, and a few hundred dollars in fees a year. In addition, the mortgage has to be insured. CMHC will no longer insure these babies, but a private insurer, GE Capital, will. Also, the mortgage terms have to be the same as the marketplace. If your RRSP has cash in it, it can also be used to be a lender to other people, and you can secure it against any Canadian real estate—residential or commercial.

Recently, Bank of Montreal chief economist Tim O'Neill and economist Peter Norman crunched some numbers to show that it could be more advantageous not to pay down your mortgage as quickly, but instead put more money into investments that over time yield higher returns. They used an example of a home bought in 1980 for $62,200 with no mortgage and sold in 1997 for $155,800. Let's say this home is owned by Mary, and she made no other investments. Mary's gain is $93,600 for an annual return of 5.4%

Now let's say that back in 1980, Mary put down $46,600 on the home—in other words, a 75% down payment—and mortgaged the rest. She invested $15,500 in the Toronto Stock Exchange 300 index. After 17 years, she cashes in the home, cashes in her investments, and pays off what's left on the mortgage. And guess what? She's ahead by another $16,000 in after-tax dollars. That's an annual return of 6% for her investment in a home and the market.

But let's say that back in 1980, Mary decided to put down only a 25% down payment of $15,500 on the home and took out a 25-year mortgage. She then invested the $46,600 in the TSE. After 17 years—when she cashes out—she's even better off. In the end, she's ahead by another $46,000 in after-tax dollars.

Economist Peter explains: "What we tried to do with this study was offer a benchmark for someone who was trying to decide whether to pay down the mortgage or invest the money." Peter concludes by saying that "a diversified approach" may yield greater long-term returns. Still, Bank of Montreal mortgage king Tom Alton and others on Bay Street, like conservative financial guru Thomas S. Caldwell, president of Caldwell Securities, Inc., caution us to be careful. We must remember that we don't want to end up carrying a mortgage worth more than the home, which could happen if real estate prices fall again.

In some provinces, like Alberta, you may be able to walk away from that debt, but you won't be able to in Ontario. In that province, if you run into trouble with your mortgage and fall behind in payments, the banks have two choices. They can sell your home by a power of sale or foreclose. The rule of thumb is that when it's a deflated market, when prices are stagnant, they'll use a power of sale. Why? Because if they sell your home for less than what you owe, they can take you to court and sue. And believe me, they'll come after whatever assets you have left to make up the difference. In the case of foreclosures, which are popular in an inflation-ridden market, the bank actually takes over the ownership of the home. And that means that if they're able to sell the home at more than what was owed on the mortgage, they—not you—get to keep the money.

THE REVERSAL GAME: MORE DICEY STUFF
One way homeowners can get at the money in their homes is through what's called a reverse mortgage. For those who have no beneficiaries and don't want to pass on their estate to their children, reverse mortgages can work beautifully. But there are pitfalls, as Victoria Branden, a widow living in Waterdown, Ontario, found out.

A reverse mortgage allows the homeowner to take anywhere from 15% to 45% of the value out of the home and invest in a lifetime annuity through a designated insurance firm. The insurance firm then makes regular income payments to the homeowner. The first to offer this product was a Toronto-based company called the Canadian Home Income Plan Corp. (CHIP). Now, both the Toronto Dominion Bank and the Royal Bank offer a CHIP reverse mortgage. Royal Bank's vice-president of deposits, Norman Light explains: "It's a financial tool that we predict will become increasingly popular as baby boomers enter their retirement years, which are longer and more active than in previous generations.

Reverse mortgages can also serve to cover the gap in retirement income many seniors are facing as a result of historically lower interest rates. Waterdown widow Victoria took out $28,000 from her mortgage-free home, so she could get a monthly income of $302. But here's what happened to her: First, rates paid on a reverse mortgage are traditionally higher than the banks' rates. Victoria was locked in for life at 13.75%. Then her financial situation changed. And after taking $9,000 out of her $180,000 home through the annuity, she decided she wanted to move.

When she asked about how she could get out of the reverse mortgage, she learned this chilling news. Her $28,000 reverse mortgage had grown to $39,000, and to get out of it, she'd have to pay that, plus an $8,000 penalty. Another option was to cash in the annuity and pay off the mortgage. Victoria was devastated: "Until two and a half years ago, I owned my home free and clear, and didn't owe a cent to anyone. Now, my home is mortgaged for $48,000 (including the penalty) with nothing to show for it but $9,000."

For Mary, 56, and her husband, Tom, 59, the outcome of a reverse mortgage was far more tragic. In the end, they lost their $300,000 lakeside home, in an attractive town north of Toronto. "In my 10 years of real estate, I've never dealt with anything quite as tragic as this," commented their real estate agent.

Mary's husband was suffering from a heart problem, and because he couldn't work, his income was cut in half. Their biggest asset was their home, and Tom had read how a reverse mortgage could help them out. They ended up re-mortgaging their home at 10.5% to take out an annuity at 11.5% that would top up their income. Their deal, through a financial planning company, was to pay it back in five years. But here's what happened. The value of their home fell because of deflation. As they approached pay-back time, the house was valued at $249,000. And after being mortgage free, they now owed $185,000. They listed the home, but could find no buyers.

"They kept telling me that they were promised they would never have to move," the agent recalled. "But then I got a call from the financial planners, saying if the money wasn't paid back, they'd sell the home under power of sale. My clients were devastated. They showed me the pamphlet which clearly stated they would never have to sell their home. They also believed that should they die, the insurance company would settle whatever was owed."

In the end, the real estate company and financial planning firm waived all commissions, and eventually the home sold for $190,000. That meant Mary and Tom could walk away without owing any money. But gone is their home. Gone are any retirement savings. And Tom still has a heart problem.

Reverse mortgages can work, especially for homeowners who may have some difficulty in meeting monthly expenses in their retirement years. But be careful and read the fine print.

Advertisements for reverse mortgages read like this:

- Continue to live in your home as long as you wish.
- Benefit from any future appreciation in the value of your property.
- Generate tax-sheltered income today.
- Use the funds without worrying about repayment during your lifetime.
- Sell, move, or rent your home at any time.

WHAT ABOUT INVESTING IN REAL ESTATE?

As I've said before, I believe it's real estate's turn to shine. And with the TSE's real estate index outperforming many others, there is proof something magical is happening. Should you get a piece of the action? Some planners believe real estate again belongs in a good financial plan, whether it's a home, investing in bricks and mortar, real estate shares—or something new on the market, called REITs (Real Estate Investment Trusts).

A REIT is a mutual fund, and the beauty of these lovelies is that you get to invest in real estate without the headaches of being a landlord. REITs can also be put in your RRSP portfolio. Homes and investment properties can't.

"You've basically got real estate with liquidity, that's the magic of the REIT," explains Christopher Dingle, chief executive of RealFund, Canada's first REIT.

Most of these funds are invested in retail properties, like shopping centres, but they can also include seniors' homes, apartment buildings, office complexes, and hotels. The main source of income is rent payments, and most of that income is passed to the unit holder in the form of distributions, where 65% to 90% of tax is deferred due to depreciation (capital cost allowance).

REITs have become real investment darlings in Canada. For example, in November 1996, there were only four REITs, plus a corporate REIT, with a total market capitalization of $1.3 billion. Yields were 5.5% to 7.5%. Only a year later, in November 1997, there were 11 REITS available, worth $3.3 billion, with yields of 7.5% to 9%. And as I write this, two new ones are coming on the market.

One is Canada's first Real Estate Income Segregated Fund, offered by Porthmeor Securities and purchased through ITT Hartford Life. "What we're doing is marrying the best of both worlds," comments Charles Taerk, principal, corporate finance with Porthmeor. The beauty of this new fund is that the principal amount invested is guaranteed.

Because of the tax advantages of REITs, Taerk recommends holding these investments outside an RRSP. "That way you get a bigger bang for your buck." The industry in Canada, though, is pushing Ottawa to change the rules so that REITs can operate like those offered in the United States. Charles explains: "In the U.S., REITs can be corporate structures offering common shares. But in Canada, they're trust units." What that means is that Canadians who own REITs face bigger liabilities than their U.S. counterparts. For example, if a Canadian REIT invested in a property that ended up a toxic waste dump, the unit holder might have to share in the responsibility of clean-up. However, the chances of that are very remote.

Americans Love Reits

South of the border, REITs have been around since 1961. From 1975 to 1996, the total assets in REITs grew from $4 billion to $72 billion, though growth has slowed somewhat in 1997. Here's how they performed from 1975 to 1996, when stacked against other investments in the United States.

Private property	+8.5%
Bonds	+9.6
Common shares	+14.75%
REITS	+16.32%

Source: NAREIT

Charles comments, "REITs are great for income, growth, and diversification." You can buy a REIT through any broker.

Linda's picks of what's hot, what's not

With changing demographics, and our technology revolution, come new real estate darlings. And new real estate dogs.

If you're investing in real estate, here's my best bet:

- Condos, especially those that cater to seniors and that have little maintenance
- Smaller but upscale homes, with all the conveniences aging baby boomers want. Location, services, maybe even a lakeview
- Communities geared to upscale executives, who work from a wired home office or fly the company jet to work

Stay away from:

- Big suburban homes squeezed into subdivisions with no room, no character

Remember:

- Location, location, location always rules.
- And God isn't making any more lakefront.

CHAPTER EIGHT

Taking Care of Business

WOMEN WITH THE GUTS TO BE THEIR OWN BOSSES

Cary Horning was beaming head to foot. It was a cold November morning in 1997, and there she was, a 40-year-old mother of five from Stoney Creek, Ontario, in downtown Toronto at the Metro Convention Centre, being rewarded for her guts to start her own business. "This is my dream come true," Cary told a jammed convention hall, where thousands attended a two-day symposium dedicated to entrepreneurs who are part of a new explosion in this country—owning and operating a small enterprise. She went on, "I feel lucky, getting an award for doing what I love."

Cary is among the first winners of the Toronto Sun Entrepreneurial Excellence Awards. An energetic self-starter, she's part of a growing breed of women who believe self-employment offers a chance to grab the brass ring or to get the most out of life. "After 13 years of working at the liquor store as a cashier and after the birth of my fifth child, I found it difficult to return to work," she explained. With a $500 capital investment from her husband, Brad, Cary opened Rocky River Advertising & Promotions on May 1, 1995. The company name, she jokes, comes from her business mascot, the family dog, Rocky, a 200-pound English mastiff.

Cary's first place of business was her 600-square-foot kitchen in her home. But her business grew so fast, she soon opened her own retail store—Rocky's Shirt Shack—some two kilometres away. Cary specializes in school clothes, like team sweatshirts, though she offers some 350,000 promotional products. "When it comes to school products, I believe as a mother of five I have a special touch," says Cary. "I customize order forms for each school after speaking to teachers, principals, parents, students, and advisory councils."

Cary's also blessed with a philanthropic touch. In 1994, she spearheaded a yellow ribbon campaign for a young boy who was diagnosed with brain cancer. The campaign raised $11,673.96 for the young lad's cancer treatment. Cary claims her mentor is school principal Kenn Kraeker, who "believed in me then, when I was taking on my first fundraising attempt." From fundraising to operating a business, Cary does have the Midas touch. Her sales grew from $7,432 in 1995 to $68,000 in 1996, with even healthier projections for 1997.

Her motto? "Work hard at everything you do. Believe in yourself, and never give up. Honesty, integrity, and hard work will pay off in the end."

Cary knows her road could be a rocky one and that like 80% of start-ups, she faces the chance of failure. But study after study show women's success rate at operating a business is good. In fact, time and time again they outscore their male counterparts. And, according to Statistics Canada, more and more women are taking care of business in this country. "While the likelihood of being self-employed has grown considerably over the last 20 years for both sexes, the rate of growth has been stronger for women," states a recent StatsCan study by analyst Geoff Bowlby. His study also showed that one-fifth of the 19% of the self-employed had a spouse who was self-employed in the same business. More than a third of the self-employed had spouses who were paid employees. His study also showed self-employed men were more likely than women to have employees.

The growth in this vibrant sector of the economy, which accounts for about 80% of all the new jobs in the country, is remarkable. Today, an unbelievable 2.5 million Canadians are self-employed. That's up from only 1.9 million in 1990. Put another way, by 1996, 18% of all workers were self-employed, compared to only 14% in 1989 and 12% in 1976. Most of the explosion is taking place in service industries. In fact, half of the self-employed operate firms in business services, trade, personal and household services. About one-quarter work in either agriculture or construction.

Why this great increase? Let's not forget that nasty word "re-engineering"—which simply means corporate downsizing or layoffs, in the name of boosting sagging profits and share values. This phenomenon was introduced by Wall Streeter Michael Hammer, and it gave little regard to the fall-out on Main Street where overly indebted consumers who lost jobs stopped buying goods. It gripped the landscape in the early years of a decade I call the "Nasty Nineties." And, unfortunately, it threw many valuable managers into another new phenomenon—the chronically unemployed.

The word "re-engineering" gives goose bumps to Rita Pardatscher and Julie Giordano. In the early 1990s, these two Thornhill, Ontario, mothers were downsized out of a job. And so, like Cary, they decided self-employment was their future. In June 1994, they came up with a novel idea—a transportation service for children. Within a year, their dream came true. Kids Limo Inc. became an incorporated business and a registered trademark. "We did our own market research," recalls Rita. "As active members of our community and mothers we knew what parents were missing—a service which would transport their children when they were not available, in a safe and reliable way."

But they realized the roadblocks would be many and their feat not easily accomplished. Still, they never gave up. Their first problem was misinformation. One arm of government was saying they didn't need a special licence to operate, while another arm said they did. "We discovered how misinformed we were by ministry and municipal officials," recalls Rita. "A public vehicle licence was needed and in order to get it we had to prove that our service was required." In short, they needed support from their customers or all their work was "down the drain." Their customers did rally behind them—big time. And the licence was granted.

The next hurdle was additional funding, so they could buy the best insurance policy. This feat, as so many entrepreneurs know, was one of the toughest. Armed with financial statements and a well-thought-out business plan, they approached several loans officers and were turned down. But again they didn't give up. Finally, they found one loans officer who believed in them. The loan was granted, and four years later Kids Limo Inc. now owns six vans and employs eight drivers. Plans are also underway to make the venture into a franchise.

These determined women say it took hard work, determination, a great staff, and support from husbands and children for their dream to come true. And, of course, it took loyal customers. These amazing ladies are also winners of a Toronto Sun Entrepreneurial Excellence Award. Cary, Rita, and Julie are fighting back. And you gotta love them.

They're part of a "revival" that is sweeping the landscape and bringing back confidence and jobs to Main Street Canada, and they're doing it in an environment where, finally, the number of business bankruptcies is starting to fall.

But still, the odds are stacked against them.

As part of my "Revival" campaign, I urge:

- Changes to securities rules so that we can make available more risk capital.
- A new federal government program I call "the Home Grown Plan," which, fashioned after the Home Buyers' Plan, would allow entrepreneurs to borrow up to $100,000 from their RRSP nest egg to start up or expand a viable business.

"This would be a real boost to our economy, and it would create jobs," agrees Bernard Wilson, a managing partner with Price Waterhouse. Like the Home Buyers' Plan, the money would have to be repaid into an RRSP in a designated time frame; however some critics argue that the high failure rate for small businesses could wipe out any retirement savings. My argument is the retirement savings may be wiped out anyway, if the person is forced to keep cashing in RRSPs. Besides, fashioned after the Home Buyers Plan, rules would include the money being repaid into the RRSP, after five years, in a 15-year time frame.

We also need a kinder, gentler banking system that wraps its brain around giving loans to our blossoming services industry, where it's tough to pledge hard assets, like trucking fleets, to get money.

Risk-takers like Cary, Rita, and Julie are our future, our economic saviours. But there is more governments can do to inspire them and give them the incentive to keep going.

It's interesting that federal Industry Minister John Manley claims that if every small business in this country hired one more person, Canada would *not* have a jobless rate. Yet governments at all levels make it tough with over-taxation and over-regulation. The $11-billion Canada Pension Plan tax grab will be toughest on these little guys, who have to pay both the employer's and the employee's share of CPP. Worse, the burden of payroll taxes, like CPP premiums, has been climbing higher and higher. And, unlike corporate income taxes, these payroll taxes have to be paid whether a firm makes a profit or not.

Yet despite these roadblocks, these gutsy folk keep going for the brass ring, and many of them are women.

WOMEN ENTREPRENEURS: THE GROWING FORCE

- Women own and/or operate 30% of all firms in Canada (more than 700,000 businesses).
- The number of women-owned businesses is increasing at more than twice the national average (19.7% for women-led firms, compared to 8.7% for all firms).
- Women generate about 40% of new start-up businesses in Canada every year, up from 30% in 1981. Projections indicate that by the year 2000, women will start 50% of Canada's new companies.
- Businesses incorporated by women more than doubled in the past 10 years compared to those incorporated by men, which increased by one-third.

- The average age of women business owners is 45. Some 79% of them are married and over half have children.
- At least two-thirds of the self-employed women start their own businesses, while one-third buy existing firms.
- One-third of self-employed Canadians are women; this has increased from 19% in 1975.

Why self-employment? A recent Royal Bank survey found this:

- The self-employed enjoy work, with 88% happy with their jobs.
- They have direction, with two-thirds using a career plan.
- They are confident, with 42% feeling "very successful."
- They possess initiative with nine out of ten claiming to have control of their jobs and schedules.

The only downside? The self-employed will likely work longer hours. They can expect to be on the job an average 43 hours a week, plus 14 hours of overtime, compared to corporate employees who'll work 40 hours and 10 hours of overtime.

Another Royal Bank survey, conducted by the Angus Reid Group Inc., found that women are 15% more likely than men to have a mentor help them start out. Women also are 25% more likely than men to have a written formal business plan, while they're 40% more likely than men to take a course, and 80% agree owning a business is "a change for the better."

But remember, the money isn't always great. According to the latest self-employment study by Statistics Canada, 45% of the self-employed in 1995 earned only $20,000, up from $15,300 in 1993. But there's still an opportunity to earn six digits. For example, in the same year, 4.2% earned more than $100,000.

Here's a sampling of 1995 earnings of the self-employed:

Self-Employed Earnings:

Occupation	1995 Employer Earnings
Natural Sciences	$56,800
Social Sciences	$103,200
Medicine	$84,700
Artistic	$37,000
Clerical	$28,500
Sales	$37,000
Service	$26,200
Farming	$23,100
Fishing	$32,700
Processing	$26,200
Machining	$29,800
Product Fabricating	$31,200
Construction	$35,400
Transportation Operating	$29,700
Other Crafts	$45,800
Personal/Household Services	$24,300

Statistics Canada

If the stakes are high, and the money may be not so hot, why are more and more women making the plunge? Experts agree that for most women, it's the independence and personal freedom that drives their desire to own their own business.

If you do decide to go ahead, here's how to get started:

First, find a niche or product that you're passionate about. Then make sure there's a market for your product or service, and get busy putting together a comprehensive business plan with all the financial details. Also, pick a name and register your business. You'll need a Business Identification Number (BIN), which costs about $70. A BIN is also needed to open a bank account. At this point, spending an extra $10 or so might be worthwhile to do a search on your company name, to ensure no one else has already registered the same name. If your service or product is subject to provincial sales taxes, a vendor's permit may be needed. Check with the local retail sales tax office. Also, check out whether you'll need a GST registration number.

Most financial institutions offer great self-help books to help you get started. They're free, so pick one up.

Linda's Secrets To Success

When it comes to running a business, common sense is likely your best guide. But here are a few tips to help you find your way:

- A business plan, with a roadmap to financial success, is key. No one, not even an angel investor, is going to get behind you without one. Use lawyers, accountants, or other professionals, if you must.
- If you expect someone to invest in your firm, then invest in it yourself.
- Don't be afraid to barter to keep overhead costs down.
- Don't let money owing to you slip into the dangerous 90-day and beyond twilight zone. Keep on top of overdue accounts.
- Remember the personal touch. In a world where technology can keep production costs down, don't forget your customers still want to know you.
- Know how to balance the books or hire a good accountant to help you. One of the best ways to find one is through word of mouth or through your banker.
- Try to establish a good relationship with suppliers, so you can buy supplies on credit.
- If you make a profit, share it. One way to keep employees motivated is to share the rewards, then watch the rewards grow even bigger.
- Know your clientele and market your stuff. A solid marketing plan is key.
- Always seek advice from a successful person, who'd like to be your business mentor. And network. There are many groups out there who meet regularly and offer seminars on home-grown businesses.
- Do research, and don't be afraid to get information. Banks and governments at every level offer free material for starting or growing a small business.
- Don't forget your family, and don't forget to have some fun.

NOT GETTING OUR FAIR SHARE

When I first met Kathy Minaker, a young, 32-year-old, bustling entrepreneur, she had given up hope. It was just weeks before Canada Day 1997.

Only a year earlier, Kathy had had the world by the tail. Why? Because this brave lady had come up with an ingenious way to market tourism right across the country, through a Kid's Travel Fun Bag. A market test in summer 1996, backed by corporate sponsors and government agencies, proved she had a winner. Her firm is It's In the Bag Promotions, a venture she began by investing $60,000 of her own money. In 1997, with promised backing from Health Canada, Kathy hoped to have her product launched in time for Canada Day celebrations. Sixty students under the Canada Works program had already been hired, and financial projections calculated a $400,000 profit by the end of the year.

Then bad luck struck. Health Canada pulled its funding, and not one bank would give Kathy the time of day. In desperation, Kathy turned to Canada's banking ombudsman, Michael Lauber. Then she turned to me. "I had given up all hope, and was meeting with a bankruptcy trustee," recalled Kathy.

In my column in the *Toronto Sun*, I wrote about her plight and pleaded for someone to come to the rescue. It wasn't long before angel investors, even people offering Kathy employment, were on the line. Lauber also called a favour from KPMG senior vice-president Blair Davidson, who'd worked on big reorganizations such as Hakim Optical and wind-ups like Consumers Distributing.

But all Kathy truly wanted was $50,000 from a bank, so she could get her production line up and running, keep her faithful assistant Goldie Watts employed, and keep her promise of jobs for 60 students. Three weeks later, hope arrived. Canada's biggest bank, the Royal, said they would review Kathy's request. By July 20, the headline on my *Sunday Sun* column celebrated Kathy's success. The Royal had come through with the money. Kathy was back in business. But she didn't stop there. She took her message to the gold-plated towers on Bay Street, where on the fortieth floor of Royal Bank's headquarters, she called together a group to talk about the problems. "If I'm having trouble, how many others out there are, too?" asked Kathy, who now has her own syndicated radio talk show for small business issues. She carefully spelled out that she was not into bank bashing, just making sure that those who deserve it get their fair share.

I think the numbers speak for themselves. In 1996, Canada's record-profit Big Six banks dished out $455 billion in business loans, with 85% of the money going to bigger corporations. Meanwhile, the little guys who were seeking only $250,000 or less and who account for 85% of the banks' business customers received only 6.9% or $34.7 billion of the money. To help the little guy, the federal government recently beefed up its Small Business Loans Act. But up to 90% of the money given out through the banks under the program is guaranteed by the federal government. In other words, if there's a default, the banks don't pick up the loss, the taxpayers do.

If you can't get funding through the banks, where else can you go?

- **Trust companies and credit unions**
- **Venture capitalists**
- **Angel investors or partners**
- **Personal assets**
- **Personal lines of credit or credit cards**
- **Leasing**
- **Merchant banks**
- **Junior capital pools**
- **Labour-sponsored venture funds**
- **Family or friends**

Never, never, though, get taken by scuzzy loan brokers who promise a business loan for an upfront fee. After the fee is paid, chances are you'll never see the money.

WHAT IF I FAIL?

Face it. More than 80% of new businesses fail within their first five years, and if the enterprise has been built by pledging personal assets, the collapse can be devastating. According to the experts, you're flirting with disaster if you fail to:

- Plan properly
- Monitor financial performance
- Understand pricing
- Monitor cash flow
- Manage growth
- Borrow properly
- Plan for transition periods

Another mistake proprietors make is failing to understand the risk they're taking. Lawyer Milton Zwicker, a small business legal expert who's from my hometown of Orillia, Ontario, reminds business owners to think about these issues:

- Customers being hurt on your premises
- A delivery vehicle accident, or the possibility that an employee may lose or damage a customer's original documents
- Storage and disposal of toxic chemicals
- Problems with a lease, and the legal and practical aspects of renewing one
- The possibility an employee will quit and open up a similar business across the street after stealing a confidential customer list.

And finally, do you seal your deals in writing or with a handshake?

"Yes, you can do business with a handshake," says Zwicker. "But in many cases agreements sealed on a handshake are difficult to prove." Zwicker adds that a law, called the Statute of Frauds, governs when an agreement must be in writing. For most business deals, this usually includes promising to pay the debt of another and the sale of land.

The guiding principle is: if in doubt, check it out.

THE TAX BENEFITS

After tax reform scaled back or eliminated many tax credits in this country, there were a few still left for the self-employed. For example, if you operate a business out of your home, you can deduct mortgage interest, property taxes, utilities, insurance, and other household costs for that percentage of space dedicated to your office. Certain travel expenses are also deductible, and if there's earned income, you can deduct other "reasonable" expenses.

"It depends on the nature of your business," comments tax accountant Steve Ranot of Marmer Penner.

And for more tax savings, if your business is earning income, you can hire the hubby (if his income is lower) or the kids, but it must be for reasonable work and reasonable pay.

Another piece of advice from Steve is that if the company is not incorporated and it loses money, the losses can be deducted against all other income. "So, if you start up a business part-time, while you earn employment income, your start-up losses will generate much-needed tax savings," says Steve.

If your business is incorporated, losses cannot be used by the shareholder, but if the business fails, the shareholder may qualify for an "allowable business investment loss"—three-quarters of which is deductible against other income. The best advice I can give is to consult a tax accountant.

Linda's Tips for Buying a Business

- Know your strengths and, most of all, your weaknesses. Don't buy a business, unless it sells something you can talk passionately about.
- Decide on the industry that excites you.
- Do some homework on the industry—for example, talk to business associations and visit your local library.
- Set the cash down payment you can raise.
- Get the support of your family and investors, if necessary.
- Review your plans with a banker
- You need a lawyer, accountant, and perhaps a business valuator. Make sure these team members have experience buying and selling businesses. They should know the key legal, tax, and other items that may affect your buying decision. You should know and discuss with your team the general pricing multiples and rates of return available in the market.
- You must determine how motivated the vendor is to sell (i.e., retirement age, medical reasons, shareholders' dispute, sell-off by a large company).
- Is the vendor "key" to the business?
- Are you being objective? Too much contact with a vendor can cloud your objectivity.
- Does the business depend on a few key customers or suppliers?
- What can you improve to make the business grow?
- What aspects of the business and industry are key to your negotiating a fair price and terms with the seller?
- Are the seller's asking price and terms within a reasonable negotiation range?
- Don't rush into an offer. Beware also of a seller or agent who says, "Trust me."
- Perform an in-depth financial statement review for the past three to five years. Compare the business ratios and trends in the business to those in the industry.

(compliments of Zwicker, Evans & Lewis)

THE OFFER

When you make an offer, put it in writing and address these issues:

- Do I purchase assets instead of shares?
- Detail seller commitments and warranties supported by your right of "set off" against holdbacks, vendor take backs or earnouts.
- Get a guarantee from the seller that you can collect the receivables and that inventory is in good condition.
- Ensure there's a vendor indemnity for employees' severance pay arising after the closing.
- Be sure the deposit is refundable until you and the vendor meet all conditions or, better still, until the closing.
- Negotiate an adjustment date prior to the closing date, if the business is profitable.
- Get a non-competition restriction covering the maximum period and geographical locations that are within legal limits.
- Have a long "subject to" period.
- Have key financial figures audited or verified to your satisfaction.
- Allocate the purchase price to expenses you can "write off" or to assets with high tax rates.
- Secure exclusivity of the negotiations, so the seller does not shop your offer.
- Be sure you have an opportunity to interview employees, key suppliers, and customers. A vendor's plea for total confidentiality may be an attempt to hide problems.
- Prior to going to the altar, check to see that you and your advisers have completed all their due diligence steps. You should not buy a business without a detailed, operational, financial, marketing, and legal review. Do not complete the purchase, if you discover material deficiencies or negative information that you cannot solve to your satisfaction.
- Remember, a divorce is more expensive than a marriage.

IS THE INTERNET FOR YOUR BUSINESS?

My friend Martha couldn't wait to set up a Web site page for her new lingerie business. And for her, it works. Customers from as far away as Japan are snapping up her sexy stuff. But the Internet can cause some high-tech headaches for small businesses. For example, it used to be that all you had to do to set up a page was find someone with a basic knowledge of the Hypertext Markup Language and you had yourself a site. Now, you need to know a host of languages, including how to use plug-ins and browser features that add sound, graphics, and video to Web sites.

But more importantly, have you done your market research? Do you know your customers? Will the Internet reach them, and will the new business generated justify the costs?

Also, who owns the copyright? You or your Web site creator? Tread carefully.

Linda's Tips to Find That Right Web Page Designer

- Make sure your designer does not breach any copyright laws.
- Make sure your contract with a designer spells out what material you must supply, when, and the format. A good site must come from the co-operative efforts of both of you.
- Your agreement should cover dates of completion of tasks, like delivery of story boards, translation of the data and graphics.
- A design contract, like any good business contract, should have a penalty clause in case the designer does not meet your deadlines.
- During design, you may divulge confidential information about your business to the designer. Cover yourself with a confidentiality clause.
- Don't let the designer own the copyright for your site. It's your money, so specify in the contract that you own the copyright.
- Remember, cyberspace is not a Wild West, lawless frontier. Copyright, trademark, defamation, and privacy laws apply. So use your good judgement.

WHERE TO GET HELP

There are plenty of places where a girl can get help to start a business. Here are a few:

The Canadian Association of Business and Professional Women's Clubs
56 Sparks St., Suite 308
Ottawa, Ont., K1P 5A9
(613) 234-7619

The Canadian Association for Home-Based Business
1200 East Prince of Wales Drive
Ottawa, Ont., K2C 1M9
(613) 724-7964

The Canadian Women's Foundation
133 Richmond St. W., Suite 504
Toronto, Ont., M5H 2L3
(416) 365-1444

Women Business Owners of Canada
A national "virtual organization," sponsored by Royal Bank and IBM
www.wboc.ca
(416) 236-2000 or 1-888-822-9262

CHAPTER NINE

The Riches in Life

ARE COLLECTIBLES, ART, GOLD BARS, VINTAGE CARS, FURS, AND DIAMONDS FOR ME?

Some girls make the fatal mistake of possessing all the trappings to give the impression of lots of money—mink coats, a Jag, diamond rings, and furnishings found only in *Homes & Garden* magazine. But when it comes to the bank account or an investment portfolio, the cookie jar is empty.

Charlene was a prime example. At 30-something, she was divorced, had no children, and as a promotional superstar was earning a great income. Char looked like money. Her wardrobe was impeccable, her company car stylish, and her lifestyle so upscale many of us would die for it. Life was great. But then she left her great promotions job and entered the world of self-employment through a franchise that flogged motivational seminars. Gone was the company car, the expense accounts, the lavish lifestyle. What money she had saved, and it wasn't much, was invested in her new venture. And as fate would have it, it was in this venture she met her husband-to-be. In the end, both left the franchise, and after tying the knot, hubby landed a prime job in Vancouver's hot real estate market. He was doing great, but Char was soon to give up work altogether. She was going to become a mom.

During a recent visit to Ontario, Char quipped, "My husband still can't believe I made all that money way back when, and all I had to show for it was an outdated fur coat that cost me a fortune. I don't even wear it any more. If I had it to do again, believe me things would be different."

Char is now back in the workforce, and a very happy mom, but instead of buying all the trappings, her money is now being invested in their new home, plus a retirement savings plan.

151

The question is, if you can afford it, should you be investing in status symbols? Some experts argue yes, if all the groundwork of a great financial plan has already been laid, and targets for a proper nest egg can easily be attained.

Art, for example, can appreciate faster than the rate of inflation. And a luxury car, properly cared for, can keep its value, compared to the run-of-the-mill new auto, which loses up to one-third of its value as you drive it off the lot. "People who have their financial lives in order and are looking for some toys or some fun after all those hard years of raising the kids are among my clients," says vintage car expert John McDonnell, who owns Arizona's Collectible Automobiles in Toronto. A recent customer is a well-to-do West Coast lady, who paid $45,000 for a 1964 Rolls Royce, which John claims was a great deal.

"This baby is worth at least $65,000," he said. "It's a James Young model with a long wheel base, and only 39 were built. It was originally made for [Great Britain's] House of Lords, and has everything, make-up mirrors, lint brushes, flower vases, the works." The car, which was sold on consignment, was owned by an heir of a deceased wealthy gentleman. "When he passed away and left the car, the heir had absolutely no interest in it." John explains the vintage car market follows the same pattern as real estate. "When real estate is hot, so are vintage cars." He estimates that in 1989, when a fever gripped the North American real estate market, that same Rolls Royce was worth about $85,000. Now, real estate is shining again, and presumably that's why the values of vintage cars are on their way up again. "The trick is to try to buy low, sell high," advises John, adding it's always best to buy restored cars and to negotiate hard.

Lovers of antique cars should also take into consideration other costs, like storage fees. But getting into this elusive market doesn't necessarily need to cost a big chunk of change. For example, John has a TR6 sportscar for sale at $16,000. But he also has a 1960 Austin Healey Sebring for $140,000. For deal seekers, kicking tires at car auctions may not be a bad idea. But do your homework. As for our rich West Coast lass, she's now in the market for a 1959 Cadillac convertible.

(And to think, years ago I owned a 1971 Triumph Spitfire, which I had painted Rolls-Royce silver grey. The problem is this Spitfire spat out more parts than I could afford on the modest salary of a young, struggling journalist. I still miss that car, and all the money I put into it. But I wonder, if I had held on, what would it be worth today? I paid a mere $1,200 for it.)

While vintage cars may be the fetish of some, gold still glitters for others, even after the Bre-X scandal. For those who still lust after gold, most experts will argue gold stocks are a far better investment than bars of the precious metal. One of the biggest reasons is that gold bars are not eligible for the RRSP tax shelter. Gold stocks, though, are. Many countries used to peg the value of their currency to the value of their gold reserves. Well, no longer. And as gold has lost its glitter, some valuable gold mining companies have been forced to close mines. Shares have taken a beating, but it's presented a time to buy for those who like gold.

This hot issue rages on, with some experts adamant gold should still be part of your portfolio. Others say they wouldn't give you a cent for an ounce of gold. Let's remember that, historically, gold has been an asset that does well in troubled times. But even with this Great Stock Market Meltdown, the glittery stuff hit new lows. Maybe it's because gold has always been viewed as a hedge against inflation. And in countries around the world, where central bankers have preached tight monetary policy, there is no inflation to speak of.

CHAPTER TEN

The Golden Rule: Girls Just Want to Have Fun

I LIKE TO THINK OF THE GIRLS AS A FUN-LOVING BUNCH. BUT IF WE SPEND ALL OF OUR TIME MAKING MONEY, WHEN DO WE HAVE FUN?

My friend Diana was forced to ask this question, when she realized life can be too short. Beautiful inside and out, Di is one of the hardest working women I know. As a husband and wife team, Di and Bruce work as sub-contractors for Canada's largest moving company, AMJ Campbell Van Lines. Di counts among her clientele some of Canada's Who's Who, a feat she's worked hard to attain and of which she is so proud.

When I first met her, she was on the job round the clock making her company a go, and often on a weekend. While my friend Lesley and I would work on our suntans and sit around the pool, Di and her hubby would be working to ensure a happy customer.

For the best of clients, Di would give each detail her personal attention and would chat about the thrill of unpacking some of the most luxurious households for some most notable names.

When she did take time to sunbathe and dip in the pool with the girls, she'd chat about how fast she was paying down the mortgage, about how much money she was socking her into RRSP portfolio, and how educational nest eggs were well underway for her two children.

But one day, Di's world caved in. At only 38, she was diagnosed with cancer of the thyroid and lymph nodes. Luckily, early diagnosis and surgery have left her with a clean bill of health. But now, she looks at life differently.

"It was the biggest scare of my life," she recalls. "I learned a lot from it. I learned that I must enjoy my family, my life and the wonderful things it has to offer now."

Di now throws all her extra change in a jar for vacations, and every year you'll find her, hubby, and the two kids enjoying a week or two in the sun in some exotic, southern location. She's also learned that she deserves special attention. A visit to the spa, a pedicure, a manicure, and other luxuries of life are no longer out of the question. But this doesn't mean Di has stopped giving special attention to her financial nest egg. *Au contraire.* Instead, she still religiously socks bucks away for the day she and hubby retire. She just spends a little of it now for a good time.

ENJOY LIFE NOW

Even my own sweet mother—who, as a Depression baby, could stretch a penny into a dollar and who scrimped and saved her whole life—knows girls just want to have fun. "I want to enjoy time with you now," she told her four daughters at a recent family reunion. Then she surprised us all by announcing she was taking the girls—Judi, Karen, Susan, and me—on a vacation. My foxy Aunt Gale would join us, too. Susan lost no time in netting a special deal through a last-minute club. Destination? Dominican Republic—here we come.

On the plane, giggling, gossiping, and just having fun—we were still pinching ourselves. Could this be true? For so many years, we laboured over our jobs, we raised our children, and we were always there to make sure the home fires were burning. We never, in our wildest dreams, imagined we could leave it all behind for a week to be together with our beautiful mother in some strange land—sunbathing, playing pool volleyball, swimming up to the pool bar for a cocktail at high noon, and stuffing our faces with exotic foods when the sun went down. It was just too good to be true. Mom, thank you. This book is for you.

HOW YOU CAN REACH ME

1. **Through my publisher, Turner Books, 1670 Bayview Ave., Suite 310, Toronto, Ont., M4G 3C2. E-mail, www.turnerbooks.com.**
2. **Through Linda Leatherdale, Money Editor, The Toronto Sun, 333 King St. E., Toronto, Ont., M5A 3X5. Phone (416) 947-2332, or fax (416) 947-2041.**
3. **Through my E-mail, lleather@sunpub.com**

Index